NOT LYING DOWN

Dear Mark,

Keep up the great work with the running!

Carole Stanley

Editor: Gillian Buckley

Design: Laurelea Conrad

Cover Photograph: ZoomPhoto.ca

Back Photo: Get to the Point Media

Library and Archives Canada Cataloguing in Publication

Slaveley, Carole
    Not Lying Down - How I Conquered Years of Pain to Triumph at the Finish Line/ Carole Slaveley

ISBN 978-0-9937181-2-0

Printed in the U.S.A.

DISCLAIMER

Any information in this book related to health and wellness is shared with the sole purpose of providing information based on the author's personal experiences. The author is not an expert on any medical condition, and the information in this book should in no way be interpreted as medical or diagnostic advice.

Always consult with your physician or other certified health professional before adopting any of the suggestions or drawing any conclusions from this book.

SPECIAL NOTE

A full distance triathlon is an event involving a 3.8 km swim (2.4 miles), 180 km (112 miles) of cycling, and a 42.2 km (26.2 miles) run, in that order. The term IRONMAN® is a registered trademark of World Triathlon Corporation. When used in this book, it refers specifically to full distance triathlon races sanctioned by the World Triathlon Corporation. The author is not affiliated with nor does she represent World Triathlon Corporation.

NOT LYING DOWN

CAROLE STAVELEY

There are two primary choices in life:
to accept conditions as they exist, or
accept the responsibility for changing them.

Denis Waitley

TABLE OF CONTENTS

Dedication:

To my dad, who taught me about integrity and doing things right. You are still with me in spirit every day of my life.

To my husband, Rod, the love of my life and my best friend. Without you, I would not be living my dream. Your support and encouragement through thick and thin have been admirable.

To my beautiful girls, Arquelle and Sabrina. You are my miracles, my treasures, and the pride of my life.

Foreword

I first met Carole more than two decades ago when she started dating my friend, Rod. They are now married. Since that time I have had the gift of her friendship.

Despite having spent countless hours with her, I got to know Carole even more while reading this book. I have no doubt that the ideas, tips, and resources that underlie what Carole presents will have a substantial impact on your fitness and health. I am honored to have been invited to write this foreword.

NOT LYING DOWN: HOW I CONQUERED YEARS OF PAIN TO TRIUMPH AT THE FINISH LINE is a remarkable story about how a woman with chronic pain competed in an IRONMAN triathlon. It is a story about how following your intuition and being an advocate for your own health can get you to inner victory.

A few years ago, Carole and I found ourselves discussing the kind of life we wanted to create. As our children grew and our lives became busier we realized that fitness and health don't just happen. It takes energy, dedication, discipline, and determination. Having a friend to call upon for support with training and to push through the pain was a true blessing for both of us. We understood each other.

Being fit without pain was hard work for Carole. On many occasions, I wished I could take away her aches and pains. It was so much more complicated for her. There were underlying issues and causes for Carole's inability to run or play tennis, but the solutions weren't clear. Those days are gone, but still to be remembered, as they were the fuel that drove Carole toward her journey in overcoming health barriers. This enlightening journey is what led her to establish Inner Victory Coaching, with the goal of guiding others toward experiencing the triumph of crossing their own finish lines.

Carole's book addresses several intriguing questions. Why do people fail to get answers for their medical concerns? Why are some health care practitioners so much better than their peers at problem solving? Why do others dismiss patients' concerns too quickly? Carole shows us that the answer is to never give up. Always trust your intuition and ask questions. Utilize your networks. Take responsibility for your own health. The payoff, as Carole shows us, is priceless.

People like Carole are unique in the health and wellness industry. Her goal is to provide guidance and support in order to make everyone their own success story.

I have followed Carole's successful career path from pharmaceutical executive to author, motivator, and coach. What I realize makes Carole so successful can be found in this book. It will provide you with the skills and answers to help you reach your highest potential, to unleash the champion within!

Carole's energy is contagious. In her presence, people come to believe that they can become fitter, healthier, and pain free. She excels at bringing out the best in people and gives you hope that your health and fitness goals can be reached.

By applying the lessons shared in this book, you can potentially take years off the search for solutions to your health concerns, so you can move forward with fulfilling your life's dreams.

I know that you will feel inspired by this book.

MT MEIKLE

Acknowledgements:

Above all, thank you to my chronic myofascial condition. Without it, I wouldn't have a story to tell, and I might never have found my calling.

Through this seventeen-year process of overcoming my body's physical limitations, there were many people who contributed not only to getting me back to full functionality, but to inspiring me to achieve higher goals. How can I thank all my friends and family members who were there for me, cheering me on no matter what I chose to pursue, whether the crazy dream of completing an IRONMAN or writing a book and starting my own business?

Mom: Thanks for always being there and for helping me become the tenacious person I am today.

MT, my closest friend, the sister I never had, my role model, and the consummate possibility seeker: Thank you for being you and for being there when I've needed you most.

Jillian Halligan, B.Sc., M.Sc., C.E.P.: How do I thank someone who gave me back my life?

Dr. Carm Stillo, Sports Chiropractor: Not only do your fantastic treatment sessions always leave me feeling better, but you've also provided reassurance and support as I've progressed from one seemingly impossible goal to the next.

Dr. Anthony Galea: For establishing the Institute for Sports Medicine (ISM) and filling it with competent, dedicated problem solvers like yourself who can truly help those of us struggling with musculoskeletal conditions.

Barrie Shepley, C3 (Canadian Cross Training Club) Head Coach: For creating a place where anyone who enjoys swimming, cycling, and/or running can be part of an inspiring group of athletes who thrive on each others' successes.

Patricia, my P&G colleague: Thank you for connecting me with your friend, Julie, who discovered a superior fertility clinic in the Colorado Center for Reproductive Medicine.

Julie: You shared your research and helped me understand the vast canyon that separates those who call themselves fertility specialists from those who truly are fertility experts. Thank you.

Dr. William Schoolcraft: Thank you for your brilliance and leadership in the field of infertility.

Rebecca Mountain, owner of Impetus Social Inc.: Thank you for helping me to understand how my journey from chronic pain to IRONMAN finisher could become a sustainable business that could improve peoples' lives. And for connecting me with Tina, my lifesaver.

Tina Iaquinta, owner of Modern Concierge: You've been the key to my productivity and have allowed me to focus on the activities that fuel my passion to help others achieve more in health and in life.

Introduction

....

Yes, I went from suffering from chronic muscle pain for thirteen years to completing an IRONMAN triathlon just four years after discovering how to manage my condition. But rest assured, **this is not a book about how to train for an** IRONMAN **triathlon.** It is far from that. The IRONMAN was *my* goal, the symbol of reaching my full physical potential despite my body's limitations. I want you to be inspired to pursue your own goals and to maximize your physical potential by overcoming and managing your physical limitations. This might look very different for each person. Maybe for you, it's walking thirty minutes without pain. For someone else it might be running a marathon or climbing Mount Everest. By learning from my experience and mindfully implementing some of the approaches that I discovered, I am certain you can improve your current health state. Today's modest physical goals could become tomorrow's victories, and who knows how far you could go?

I didn't write this book to put the spotlight on myself; I've never been comfortable in the spotlight. I wrote this book to give others hope that they might one day be able to feel the overwhelming sense of joy and gratitude I now feel every day of my life. I believe I never could have felt the depth of these emotions had it not been for the pain, discomfort, and desperation I felt for all those years of unknowingly suffering from chronic myofascial pain syndrome. Although the suffering was necessary in allowing me to feel a higher level of joy and appreciation for milestones as small as a few hours without symptoms and as big as completing an IRONMAN triathlon, there was no need for *thirteen years* of suffering!

So why, after finally overcoming the suffering from muscle pain, did I take on an IRONMAN triathlon? A few people who really don't understand the power of overcoming adversity and reaching higher goals have asked me: "Why would you do that to yourself?" The answer to that question is pretty complex, but let me attempt to answer it:

1. To make up for the thirteen years when I couldn't be as physically active as I wanted;

2. To see how far I could push myself once I was feeling better;

3. Each triathlon I've completed since my first (short) one in 2009 filled me with increasing satisfaction, and I wanted to keep building on those feelings with each increase in distance;

4. My IRONMAN training was a continuation of my determination to never give up, even when you can't see your way out of a tough situation;

5. I wanted to show my kids that with "stretch goals" and perseverance, you can achieve things you never dreamt possible;

6. I wanted to use the accomplishment as a vehicle for getting my message out and giving hope to others who were in the physical and mental place I was in many years ago; and

7. In my own way, I wanted to show my Dad (whom I lost in 2005), that I was okay...in fact, I was *more* than okay: I did an IRONMAN triathlon!

I hope you enjoy my story and pay attention to the lessons learned, references, and resources, which are intended to help you reach a better health state in a much shorter time than I did. I wish you much success on your journey to becoming your own health champion.

1

HOW DID I GET HERE?

Someone pinch me. Isn't this one of the races I've seen on TV that only "superhuman" athletes could possibly complete? What am I doing here? Okay, just remember, Carole: you can do the 3.8 km swim, you can do the 180 km bike, and you can do the 42.2 km run (even if it has to be a combination run/walk). Don't think about the fact that you've never done all three on the same day! Your goal is to be under 15 hours, but you have 17 hours if you need them. In order to qualify as a finisher, you just need to complete the swim in under 2 hours and 20 minutes (should be fine, as long as you don't cramp or have other issues), get off the bike before 5:30 p.m. (which gives you about 8.5 hours after getting out of the water—shouldn't be a problem without a flat tire, crash, or other issue), and then you're home free...as long as you cross the finish line by midnight.

I'm in Mont-Tremblant, Quebec. It's 6:25 a.m. on August 18, 2013, and I'm participating in the Subaru IRONMAN® North American Championship. Some of the best triathletes in the world are here. The sun is just coming up as the mayor of Mont-Tremblant welcomes everyone. The announcers begin talking about the professional triathletes who will be going in the first wave at 6:35 a.m. There are 2,600 athletes and 2,000 or more spectators on the beach, which is pretty close to full capacity. I find the sign indicating "Women 35+" and identify a spot that I think will be the back of the pack. Many women in my wave are in the water, warming up. Not me. I know my swim will be slow and steady, and I don't need to get warmed up for a faster start. And the term *warm-up* is a bit of a mis-nomer this early in the morning. The air is pretty cold, and I don't want to be shivering while I wait for my turn to get into the water. I step on an uneven section of sand in my bare feet and—*Oh, what was that?*—feel a tweak just in front of my left ankle. *Is it something to worry about? No, don't worry. It will be okay. Your body is not the same as it used to be. You're strong now. Relax: everything will be fine. Enjoy this moment; even if it is all you get to experience of an* IRONMAN *event, just being here is the greatest victory of your life.*

Around 6:32, Royal Canadian Air Force jets fly above, saluting us and the daunting challenge we are about to take on. I put on my bathing cap and place my goggles on top of my head. At 6:35, a cannon goes off in concert with fireworks, signalling the start of the professional men. A new round of fireworks goes off every three minutes to signal the start of the next wave. My husband and daughters find me and give me one last round of high-fives and hugs. My wave is last: our start signal goes off at exactly 7:00 a.m. With 600 or so women in my wave, it takes a few minutes before I actually get into the water, let alone start swimming. I'm strangely calm and relaxed, recalling many ear-lier triathlons when just the thought of the open water swim sent my heart rate soaring.

The forecast calls for a mainly sunny and hot day. The water of Lake Tremblant is calm yet shimmering with the reflection of the newly risen sun. The Laurentian Mountains stand tall in the background. I'm now about waist deep in the water. Lots of women my age are diving in and are ready to start their journey, whatever their reasons for attempting this awesome challenge. It becomes my turn to dive in and start my unimaginable day. I feel an almost eerie sense of calmness, despite the dozens of arms waving around me, a few hands hitting me. All I can see is the water; all I can hear is the counting in my head that I use to keep myself focused. On every twelfth stroke, I look toward the first orange buoy, then the next. *You can do this all day long. It won't be fast, but you know you can do it.* Then the positive and upbeat lyrics from will.i.am's "#thatPOWER" enter my head: "I'm loving every second, minute, hour, bigger, better, stronger, power...I've got that power." *What a great day for an* IRONMAN. *What a great day to start a new chapter of my life. I am so fortunate. I am free. I want others to feel this. I don't want anyone suffering more than they need to.*

It is really difficult to believe that just four years ago I was in my initial consultation with an exercise physiologist describing the frustration I'd been experiencing with muscle pain and stiffness over the previous thirteen years. The discussion brought me to tears. As much as I had always wanted to be an athlete, I had been unable to achieve the level of activity and fitness I had wanted. A soft tissue injury sidelined me in 1996, and a chronic muscle condition set in soon after that. Understanding what I now understand, I know that I would have been back to almost 100 per cent within a year of the injury had I received proper treatment. Instead, I spent many of what should have been my prime athletic years in pain, discomfort, and frustration, struggling to figure out what was wrong with me, and trying to find solutions that would allow me to return to being as athletic as I wanted to be without causing further injury and more pain and stiffness.

A strange twist of fate resulted in my finding out about a leading edge sports medicine clinic. My close friend had a remarkably fast recovery from a torn ligament after receiving treatment from a clinic her brother was affiliated with. She suggested that I go talk to someone at the clinic about my chronic problems. Following a few consults and conversations with some of the health professionals at the clinic, I was introduced to Jillian Halligan, M.Sc., Certified Exercise Physiologist. Although there were many steps involved in my eventual recovery and ability to manage my condition, meeting Jillian was probably the most important step in my journey from chronic pain and fear of injury to IRONMAN participant. During my initial consultation with Jillian, I shared with her my ultimate goal of being able to run 5 kilometers, maybe a few times a week, without being stopped by pain or a new injury.

It took more than thirteen years of searching and close to a hundred health professional visits before I found the right help, allowing me to get to where I am now at age forty-seven. As grateful as I am for having discovered solutions and being able to now manage my condition, I want to make sure you have all the information you need *now* to help you reach a better health state sooner rather than later. I am 99 per cent certain that whatever your current health problem(s), you can obtain better care, regain hope for a better future, and get more out of life than you believe possible. It starts with taking control of your health care, becoming informed about your condition, using specific guidelines to search for the right health care professionals, asking a lot of questions, and never, ever giving up. My objective with this book is to provide you with some guidance and direction that can dramatically increase your chances of getting the right help for your health condition, thereby shortening your suffering time and giving you a chance to achieve physical goals you can only dream of right now.

It is my hope that, by pulling together all the information I've learned about taking charge of my own health during my seventeen-year journey from chronic pain to IRONMAN finisher, this book benefits you. I will also share examples of other encounters within the health care system, where my and others' use of self-advocacy meant the difference between accepting a suboptimal health state and arriving at a satisfying health outcome. While it took me thirteen years of trial and error and another four years of more of methodical searching to gather all this information, I truly hope you can apply it to your current situation and reach a better health state much sooner. And then, who knows? Once you feel better, you might find the courage to start setting more and more challenging goals for yourself. I hope with all my heart that you can get to a point where a little voice in your head says: *Just maybe I can.* When you hear that voice, it means you're making progress and you believe there is hope for a brighter tomorrow. Follow that voice, set the goals, continue to apply the health advocacy insights I provide you in this book, and you'll be amazed how far you can get.

As you read through my story of going from chronic pain to competing in an IRONMAN triathlon, you'll notice that at the end of several chapters I provide an overview of my lessons learned and convey real life examples of health champions in action—people taking control of their health care. The "lessons learned" sections review some key insights that, if understood at the time that I lived them, could have significantly shortened my suffering time. The expression "hindsight is 20/20" applies here. Please use my hindsight *proactively* to turn yourself into a health champion. Unless you really believe you're at 100 per cent of your physical potential, what do you have to lose?

Appendix I reviews the nine key steps to becoming your own health champion and reaching your physical potential. It organizes all of the insights from the "Lessons Learned" into a nine-step process to guide you through truly being in charge of your health. As you read through each step, ask yourself whether you've truly explored all of your options. Are you championing your own health, or are you selling yourself short?

Appendix II provides a number of references and resources that you can turn to as you search for the right health professionals, the right questions to ask, and some inspiration to persevere.

2

FROM AVID ATHLETE TO "WHAT'S HAPPENING TO ME?"

From a young age, I was encouraged to participate in athletics. My parents did not believe in sitting around watching TV. Over time, I adopted this philosophy as my own, since it suited my personality. In addition to becoming a running and workout fanatic, I became an avid tennis player, ultimately becoming part of my university's varsity team in 1984. I loved playing competitive matches, whether with the team or independently in provincial level tournaments. After earning two university degrees, I entered the workforce in 1991 and continued to spend most of my time outside of work either exercising, running or playing tennis. My husband, Rod, whom I met during varsity tennis tryouts in 1984 and married in 1992, was the same way. I never could have married anyone who wasn't into sports and fitness.

Looking back, there were signs that I might have a chronic myofascial condition. A few times in my twenties I developed a lot of stiffness in my legs and described it to my doctor as feeling like my muscles were too short for my body. Also in that decade, I suffered a few episodes of pulling my back and my neck, again developing a very stiff feeling up and down on the injured side of my body. The underlying feeling of stiff muscles gradually increased as I approached thirty. The more running I did, the more issues I would develop, such as iliotibial (IT) band syndrome, causing pain in my knee and inflamed Achilles tendons. Being young, however, these things would eventually resolve themselves and never caused much more than a few weeks of suffering.

In June 1996, soon after we returned from a fantastic trip to Spain, Portugal, and France, I was playing tennis with a good friend and ex-varsity team member. When it started to rain, we decided to keep playing until it was too slippery to play. How did we find out it was too slippery to play? My left leg slipped out to the side as I reached for a wide ball, and I fell hard. It didn't seem too bad at the time, but over the next few days I realized something was wrong in the area of my left hip and low back. The whole area was becoming stiffer by the day, and I was feeling a lot of pain when sitting for any length of time. After a few weeks of rest, I tried to play tennis again. As I started to move around the court, I felt a shooting pain in my hip and had lots of stiffness hampering my movement.

Having always been one to solve my own problems, I didn't even think about speaking to a doctor about the issue until several weeks went by and the stiffness and pain had spread up and down my entire left side. By this point, every position, whether vertical or horizontal, was uncomfortable. I started to sleep in the guest bed so as not to disturb Rod with my tossing and turning.

I had already taken several days off work and was struggling through my days at the office. Although I was uncomfortable in all positions, sitting was by far the worst. How could I continue working at a job that involved desk work and a lot of travel? My boss offered me the option of taking a medical leave of absence, but I knew myself too well. I knew that if I took a leave, I would sink into a state of feeling even more useless and helpless. Luckily I had established myself as a reliable contributor in my first nine months with this company, and my boss told me I could work from home for as long as I needed. Thank goodness laptops were becoming mainstream in corporate offices at that time. I stacked mine on a pile of books at the kitchen table so I could work standing up.

My search for medical help started at this point. After our move to Georgetown, Ontario, in 1994, we had been too busy to find a family physician, so I started with a walk-in clinic. The general practitioner sent me for x-rays. Since the x-rays revealed nothing, he sent me home with some anti-inflammatory drugs and told me I would be fine. Another week passed with no improvement. I wasn't even driving, as it was too uncomfortable to sit. My parents came to help. They would drive me, lying down in the back seat, to my fitness club so I could at least do some water walking as exercise.

I went back several times to the walk-in clinic and was referred to several specialists who in turn sent me for many tests. The orthopedic surgeon looked at the x-rays and ordered a bone scan. According to him, there was nothing wrong with me. The rheumatologist did some blood work and ruled out all the rheumatological conditions. He also proclaimed me "fine" and sent me home with more anti-inflammatory pills, which he tried to convince me were different from the previous pills I was given. As it turned out, the pills were marketed by my employer, Procter & Gamble, and I knew all of the science behind them. There was nothing special about these pills, just more anti-inflammatories. I guess the rheumatologist thought my problem was psychosomatic, and that convincing me the pills had special powers would result in a placebo effect. That left me feeling betrayed and skeptical when it came to the medical community.

Six weeks after the injury, I still had no answers and was working part time from home, either standing up or lying down. I was in tears at least once a day, and was scared that life as I knew it was over. I started to drink a bit too much to temporarily ease the pain and stiffness (or at least try to forget about it). I lost my appetite and fell into a depression. It's a good thing I had Rod to help keep my spirits up and force me to eat some healthy foods now and then. He did so much for me, even shaving my legs since it hurt to bend forward or twist. I loved him so much for being there, yet I was so jealous of his ability to keep working out, run, and play tennis. When I look back I sometimes wonder what kept him around. I'm pretty sure my charming personality didn't shine through during that period!

I reached out to several friends for advice and direction, including my uncle, a physician who had suffered from various musculoskeletal issues himself. I tried to find a regular family doctor instead of relying on the walk-in clinic. The first doctor I found who was accepting new patients pretty much told me there was something wrong with my head since the cause of my pain and stiffness wasn't showing up on any diagnostic tests. This woman obviously did not know me. The last thing I wanted to do was invent an ailment so I could lie around all day and not play my beloved tennis or go running to burn off excess energy. God did I miss being active. I absolutely HATE lying around, and I HATE being stiff and uncomfortable. *Why can't someone help me?* I thought. *Aren't doctors trained to help people?*

At the end of three months, I found myself still unable to sit for any period of time. Every minute was uncomfortable, whether I was sitting, standing, lying down, or moving. It felt like I had a steel wire running from the left side of my neck all the way down to my left calf. I kept asking myself, now what?

Chapter 2—Looking Back: Lessons Learned

✓ Don't leave an injury or problem untreated. Deal with it right away. Be aggressive and persistent early on in your search for answers. Things can go from bad to worse if left untreated.

✓ Identify one competent health professional as the "coordinator" of your care. I started out with a walk-in clinic and jumped around to various health professionals, which didn't help in building an overall picture of my condition.

✓ If the problem is musculoskeletal in nature (muscle, soft tissue, bone), look beyond your general practitioner as soon as possible. Look for health professionals who specialize in musculoskeletal issues, such as sports medicine doctors, chiropractors, osteopaths, and exercise physiologists.

✓ If your primary symptom is stiffness, do whatever you can to keep moving. Being immobile is the worst thing you can do; it will just lead to more stiffness.

Chapter 2—Health Champion in Action

Crippling Back Pain

One day in 2012, I called to touch base with my brother Jehan, and he told me that he was suffering from a really sore back after lifting a heavy object. In fact, it was so sore that he was staying home from work that day. Being on contract, he was not getting paid for this sick day; this told me that he was in a lot of pain and discomfort. I asked what steps he had taken so far to try and resolve it. When the injury happened, he went to a walk-in clinic and got prescriptions for anti-inflammatories and physiotherapy; he had already completed a few sessions of physiotherapy with no improvement. In fact, he felt like it was getting progressively worse.

Based on my experience with musculoskeletal issues, I convinced him that he needed to see someone who specializes in this type of problem. I had an appointment booked with my chiropractor, Carm, that day and offered it to Jehan. He lives in the city and doesn't have a car, so I convinced him to rent a car for the day. When he presented his symptoms and the history of how the injury occurred, Carm knew exactly what the problem was. After one treatment, Jehan told me he felt 50 per cent better and dubbed Carm "The Magician." He was given some specific exercises to do at home, and Carm recommended one or two more visits for chiropractic treatment. In one day, Jehan was back to functioning well enough to work and carry on with activities of daily living. Within two weeks he was back to 100 per cent. Jehan was also told that the exercises recommended by the physiotherapist were exactly the opposite of what he needed to fix this particular problem.

A couple of lessons were learned in this case:

1. When dealing with musculoskeletal pain, find a practitioner who specializes in this area. Even then, you still have to ensure you have the right practitioner who uses his/her knowledge effectively to help you solve your problem. General practitioners receive very little training in musculoskeletal issues.

2. Sometimes the solution involves upfront costs. Jehan had to spend a total of about $300 in car rental and chiropractor fees for three visits. Considering his suffering and unpaid time away from work while he was doing the wrong exercises, was it worth it? I'll let you answer that one for yourself.

3

A GLIMMER OF HOPE

After visits to several doctors, one of them suggested trying some physiotherapy and gave me a referral note. I decided to go to the physiotherapy clinic right next to my gym, which I was now using for the pool, hot tub and massage therapy services instead of the tennis and workout facilities. The clinic's two therapists agreed that there was no way I should still be so stiff and in so much pain three months after sustaining the injury. After a few weeks of working with them, I was seeing some progress. They initially focused on specific stretches that gave me some instant (albeit short-lived) relief. Then they moved to exercises intended to strengthen the muscles around the hips, which were quite weak, especially on the injured side. These exercises were so difficult and uncomfortable for me that I soon gave up the most difficult ones and focused primarily on stretching, which gave me short-term relief.

This was a key opportunity for me to regain mobility and limit the widespread pain and discomfort that was taking hold of my body. The physiotherapists were guiding me in the right direction, but I didn't understand enough to know that I needed to keep up with *all* the exercises they prescribed, not just the ones that were easier or more comfortable. This whole concept of using exercise, movement, and discomfort to treat something stiff and painful was counterintuitive. I needed someone to pound it into my head over and over again. But this didn't happen and I was left to my own (ineffective) devices. Misguided beliefs about mainstream medicine were so ingrained in me that I kept looking for the "magic bullet." It would take me thirteen years to realize it did not exist.

After working with the physiotherapists for a few months and doing at least part of what they recommended, I gradually re-gained some range of motion. As I look back I realize that in-creased movement alone was probably responsible for the ma-jority of my improvement, as modest as it was. Nonetheless, I was encouraged and set a goal to be able to get on a tennis court by February 1997 to coincide with a trip to Hawaii with Rod.

Eight months after my initial injury, I did meet my goal of getting on the tennis court in Hawaii. I was so happy to be on vacation again. It was our first since my injury in June 1996. We did a lot of walking, which was frequently interrupted by my stretching breaks. During those ten or so days, I moved more than I had in the last eight months, and it felt great. We hiked up the volcano on the Big Island, went snorkeling, whale-watching, sightseeing, and saw the sunrise from Mount Haleakala on Maui. I was starting to gain an appreciation for simply being alive and able to function. This was quite a shift for someone who had always been the Type A personality for whom a two-hour singles tennis match didn't even count as a workout. I started to put life into perspective, started to prior-itize and spend fewer hours at the office. Initially I shortened my days because it was so uncomfortable to sit, but over time I realized I could still accomplish a lot in fewer hours by focusing on the important stuff.

Although my body was not at all where I wanted it to be, I began to realize that for the most part, I felt better when mov-ing rather than not. Strenuous and repetitive movements like tennis were sometimes okay but often too much. As I learned later, the answer was not to avoid the activity, but to properly train the body to be able to tolerate it.

I was eventually able to play tennis again on a fairly regular basis, but not to the level I had reached previously and only on days when I didn't feel like my muscles were going to snap. I was always tired at the thought of getting on the court, since it required so much energy just to manage the muscle stiffness. I would usually spend as much or more time on my pre-match preparation as I did on the tennis match itself. The preparation often involved a hot bath, about an hour of stretching and/or rolling on a tennis ball, and a bit of warm-up time on a stationary bike or elliptical trainer. I started thinking this was my new reality. Stuck in a stiff and uncomfortable body, but unwilling to give up on the activities I loved, I would keep participating to the degree that I could even if it meant hours of preparation and post-workout recovery and discomfort. The only "tools" I had to help me get through the day were stretching, rolling on a tennis ball, and taking hot baths. These provided just enough help to get me through the day.

I was now back at work full time and trying to remain as active as I could. My whole body was so stiff that a good part of my workday was focused on finding a private place to do some stretching and get some temporary relief. Often, it was in a toilet stall. I was frequently spotted doing neck circles while sitting at the computer or having one leg up on my desk doing a hamstring stretch. Needless to say, I didn't often wear skirts to work!

This was also when I started noticing that my muscles and soft tissues were somewhat lumpy in the places where I felt most of the discomfort. I began hearing strange popping and cracking sounds coming from my muscles (at least I assumed it was my muscles) whenever I stretched or moved in certain ways.

In late 1997, a colleague recommended a sports medicine clinic next door to the office, so I went to see the doctor there. He recommended some medications and referred me to physiotherapists. The doctor himself wasn't particularly helpful, but one of the better physiotherapists showed me a hip strengthening exercise. When I said that the exercise wasn't comfortable, he suggested that, with soft tissue problems, sometimes it might feel worse before it feels better. I wish I had believed him and taken his advice to heart. I did the exercise a few times and stopped. Again, this could have been a pivotal moment for me, but there were three factors working against me:

1. I wasn't ready to accept the message that it was okay for an exercise to feel uncomfortable.

2. The physiotherapist didn't emphasize the importance of point #1, so I didn't place much weight on it.

3. No one had begun to assess the underlying factors that were causing my soft tissues to remain stiff and sore for so long. I'm convinced that continuing with the uncomfortable strengthening exercises alone would have improved my situation. However, without addressing the systemic issues, my progress would have been limited.

There were a few other glimmers of hope and missed opportunities with the sports medicine clinic. One of the physiotherapists would apply pressure to the piriformis, one of the muscles in spasm in my hip area, while moving my leg at the same time. I know now that this technique is called "active release," but it was not well known at the time. This particular physiotherapist had simply discovered that this approach seemed to give people a lot of relief when the hip area was locked up. It did seem to really help, but for some reason I didn't pursue it with any energy. I guess I was still subconsciously looking for the big bang of success. I felt that when I found "the answer," I would know it, and all the pain and stiffness would subside permanently. Until then, I was resigned to a less than optimal life. Sound familiar?

So I continued the struggle of trying to function in a less-than-optimal body, stretching at every opportunity and avoiding sitting whenever possible. In fact, whenever I had a few moments to relax, I found myself on the floor of my family room either rolling on a tennis ball or stretching. It would be a long time before I found myself sitting on a couch again. I guess that meant less wear and tear on our family room furniture!

I was often very tired, as it was difficult to find a comfortable position in which to fall asleep. I would kiss Rod good night around 11 p.m., and then begin my ritual of stretching and rolling that could last anywhere from twenty minutes to more than two hours, depending on how I felt that day. It was really difficult to predict the degree of pain and discomfort I would have in any given day.

Despite the physical discomfort, I did enjoy my work. My career with Procter & Gamble Pharmaceuticals was flourishing. My husband Rod and I had always been interested in travel and exploring new places, so when an opportunity for me to transfer to Cincinnati, Ohio, arose in 1998, we accepted it.

Those were fun days. We spent six months in temporary housing, acquired a second cat, and bought a new house that felt like a mansion to us since the cost of living in Ohio was much lower than in Ontario. During those first six months in Cincinnati, Rod couldn't start his new job because of immigration bureaucracy, so he had dinner on the table for me almost every night, took care of the house, and had the time to train for his first marathon. It was so exciting to cheer him on at the Ottawa marathon. I wished I could do something like that some day, but I was beginning to accept my new life, which did not include long distance, high-level or high-intensity athletic undertakings.

In addition to playing tennis, I ran short distances whenever I could, always testing how far I could go without an injury occurring. Quite consistently, I would get into trouble when I reached distances around 5 km. So the time between runs was usually quite long; I often went months without attempting a run as I recovered from injuries or feared the next injury. The same went for tennis. I would play as hard as I could as long as I wasn't injured. But injuries occurred pretty regularly, which meant several weeks off to recover. When new injuries happened, only the new problems were addressed by the medical community and not the underlying chronic cause.

Chapter 3—Looking Back: Lessons Learned

✓ If a potential solution seems to be helping, implement *all* of the recommended steps, and keep looking for more solutions along the same lines. It's likely that the complete solution involves more than one approach.

✓ If a treatment or potential solution is difficult or uncomfortable, think twice before abandoning it, especially if someone can explain to you why it is beneficial. Those things that don't provide short-term relief could be long-lasting resolutions to your problem.

✓ Remain open to accepting and implementing new solutions.

✓ Find ways to keep moving, especially if your problem involves soft tissues. No matter what your condition, lack of movement will often cause more problems than it can fix.

✓ Set goals related to activities you love (e.g., getting back on the tennis court by a certain date).

Chapter 3—Health Champion in Action

My Baby Needs Surgery!

From the time she was born, Lisa's daughter sounded congested; everyone had an opinion as to what the cause might be. The baby had a constant runny nose, which was not adequately addressed by her pediatrician. At about four months, Lisa took someone's suggestion and saw a naturopath about the problem. Because Lisa was breastfeeding, the naturopath suggested that she change her diet to cut out dairy, wheat, and sugar. Left to her own devices in implementing this change, Lisa did not understand that she needed to find nutritious substitutes for the foods that she removed from her diet in order to keep her body strong and healthy. After a few weeks of avoiding just about everything, she lost weight, felt lethargic, and gave up.

The general practitioner, the ear, nose, and throat specialist, and the surgeon all agreed that the problem was due to the baby having a blocked nostril, which could be fixed with surgery. A bit reticent to agree to surgery, Lisa asked a common-sense question that none of the doctors could answer: "Where is all the mucus coming from?" Determined to get to the bottom of it, she decided to meet with another naturopath recommended by a friend. He changed her life. Although he said a lot of the same things as the first naturopath, he gave her concrete direction on what to eat and provided better explanations. Once Lisa understood the underlying relationship between food and her daughter's symptoms, it was easy to make changes in her family's eating plan. She saw a significant improvement in her daughter's symptoms in a short time, and these new insights led her to do her own research and to find additional solutions, which took her even further in establishing a healthy nutritional plan for the whole family.

The key lessons revolve around searching until you find someone who can answer your questions in a satisfactory manner. You need to consistently do your own research and remain committed to finding solutions that work for you.

MY INFERTILITY STORY

Overcoming infertility to ultimately give birth to my two beautiful daughters was the first significant step in my eye-opening journey to becoming my own health champion.

In late 1997, after more than five years of marriage, Rod and I decided we might want to have children. We weren't 100 per cent sold on the idea, but thought we would take the plunge by removing birth control from the equation and seeing what would happen. We were birth control free for about six months when I was offered my transfer to Cincinnati. At that point, we decided to put the baby making on hold so I could settle into the new job. By late 1998, we went back to no birth control and expected that, at any time, I could become pregnant. It's strange how the whole baby-making process morphed into a goal achievement exercise. I was someone who always believed that if you want something, you do what it takes until it happens. The same goes for a baby, right? When ten months went by without any success, I was getting very frustrated. Recall that I didn't want a baby that badly at first. But when the powers that be were telling me it might not happen, I went into rebellion mode. No one will stop me from obtaining something I want!

A good friend who had been through a long infertility struggle before giving birth to twins encouraged me to start the process of speaking to an infertility specialist. I booked an appointment with the local physician who had helped her.

The first step for me was to undergo exploratory surgery. It suggested some mild endometriosis, but not enough to cause infertility. In addition, Rod had a sperm analysis. These invasive steps really didn't bother either of us. We were now focused on achieving our common goal, the drive for which trumped whatever sentiments existed early on about the prospect of having babies.

At that point I started taking clomiphene, a drug that is supposed to regulate ovulation and increase the odds of pregnancy. I was warned that clomiphene can have some psychological and emotional side effects, but I was not prepared for what it brought. I turned into a crazy person. One night as I was lying in bed, I heard a sound coming from outside and remembered we had left the windows open in order to let in the fall breeze. For some reason, I ran downstairs in a fit of rage and started to slam all the windows shut. Rod was a bit taken aback by my behavior, but he didn't criticize, accuse, or ask questions. He was just there for me, supportive as always. On another occasion, I was playing an inter-club tennis match and had a complete meltdown after missing one too many forehands. I went up to the net, told my opponent I wasn't feeling well and forfeited the match. I had never done that in my life. After two or three months of this craziness, I put an end to the clomiphene and asked about other options.

The next step, I was told, was to take injectable fertility medications and follow that with an intrauterine insemination. The fertility medications would induce ovulation on a specific day, at which time the sperm is collected and placed in the uterus with a sort of "turkey baster" syringe. We went through this process twice with no success. My doctor also suggested that I cut out caffeine, gain a few pounds, and try to reduce stress, all of which I did.

By this point, I was beginning to feel betrayed by my body. In other aspects of life, we can take certain obvious steps to get what we want or live with the consequences of not taking those steps. For example, if I wanted good grades in school, I studied. If I didn't study enough, I got lower grades than I wanted, but I could accept responsibility because I didn't do my due diligence. In the case of trying to get pregnant, there was so much outside of my control. I was doing everything I could with no results to show for the effort. This was very frustrating. And having to wait twenty-eight days between answers was excruciating. Patience is not one of my virtues under the best of circumstances.

Once the minimally invasive steps had failed, the doctor suggested that we needed to move on to in vitro fertilization to improve our odds of success. Since this would be a significant time and money commitment, I wanted to give it the best possible chance of success by reducing the stress associated with the process. So I approached my boss about taking a leave of absence to focus on this in vitro attempt. He was incredibly supportive, and I was granted a three-month unpaid leave.

Over the course of the first two weeks of the in vitro cycle, there were many visits to the laboratory for blood work and ultrasounds and several daily self-injections. Then the day came for the egg retrieval. While I was under a general anesthetic, the doctor went in through the uterus to retrieve the eggs from my ovaries. As in every single procedure I underwent in our attempt to conceive, Rod was there waiting for me as I woke up from the anesthetic. The retrieved eggs were placed in a petri dish and the sperm added to them to allow for fertilization (thus the name "in vitro fertilization"). After a few days, a number of embryos were formed and began to develop. I then returned to the clinic for the embryo transfer procedure. The best two or three embryos were placed into my uterus in the hopes that at least one would become implanted in the uterine wall and begin to grow. We even got a picture of our embryos before they were transferred.

I had read that some clinics would encourage patients to spend a few days on bed rest following the embryo transfer. When I asked my fertility specialist about this, her response was "implantation is not a function of gravity." I didn't do anything crazy for the next two weeks, but I did not stay off my feet. At the end of two weeks, the moment of truth came. A blood test was done to determine whether or not the procedure had been successful—was I pregnant?

It was devastating to receive the answer from my doctor's office. The procedure had not been successful. Since I still had about six weeks off work, we were prepared to go right back in there and try again. And we did. We repeated the exact same process, feeling confident this time would be the successful one. After all, we were doing everything right and following all instructions to a T. How could we not succeed? Well, everything was an exact replica of the first attempt, including the negative result. This time, the pregnancy test was done from a clinic in Hilton Head, North Carolina, where we had taken a short vacation before I returned to work. These results were even more difficult to accept the second time around. I went into a depressed state. Rod was incredible through it all. I know it was difficult for him too, but his promise to me was "We'll just keep trying until..."

On our follow-up appointment with our fertility specialist, she suggested that, at thirty-four years old, my eggs were probably not of the best quality, and that I should consider moving to an egg donor program. I got the impression that she was guessing at this diagnosis, so I asked a question that I felt needed to be answered before jumping to the conclusion that my eggs were no good: "How do we know whether an embryo can actually implant into my uterus?" To this, the doctor replied: "There is no way to determine that, and even if we could, it would not change our course of action."

This did not sit well with me. Not only was I unsure about using someone else's eggs, but I was really skeptical about jumping into a procedure that would cost twice as much as the previous two without knowing that an embryo could actually implant itself into my uterus. We decided to take a step back and re-evaluate our options for achieving parenthood.

The following month or so was emotionally difficult. Not only were we beginning to face the fact that we might never have babies biologically, but it appeared as though adoption could be nearly impossible as well. Not being US citizens, we were not eligible for an international adoption through the US. And not being Canadian residents, we were not eligible to adopt as Canadian citizens. We were not keen on a local adoption, which we were told would be "open." This would mean that the biological mother could have access to our adopted child in the future, which didn't sit well with us.

I had developed some great friendships with the women on my team at work, and it helped to be able to share with them what was happening to me. One day, Patricia, one of my closest friends on the team, said, "You need to talk to my friend Julie. She just had twins after several failed in vitro attempts here in Cincinnati. She did some research and ended up going to a clinic in Denver where she succeeded on her first attempt." So Patricia connected me with Julie, who was very happy to share what she had learned on her journey. I met her and her beautiful babies and followed all of her advice down to every detail.

Julie started by pointing me to the Centers for Disease Control and Prevention (CDC) online audit of assistive reproductive technology clinics across the US. This audit compared success rates in an apples-to-apples format for just about every clinic in the country conducting in vitro fertilization. My eyes nearly jumped out of their sockets when I looked at the data. The gap between the least successful and most successful clinics in the country was close to 50 per cent. Yes, that's 50 per cent! In looking at the percentage of embryo transfers that resulted in pregnancy, the success rate ranged from around 15 per cent at the least successful clinic to 65 per cent at the most successful. What was going on? How could all these doctors call themselves fertility specialists? The Cincinnati clinic where I had undergone the two in vitro procedures had a success rate in the 30 per cent range. What the hell was I doing? I wanted to be at the clinic with a 65 per cent success rate!

Something that Julie also pointed out to me was the fact that the clinic in Denver seemed to do a lot of things differently. They were pioneers in the field: the ones doing the research and coming up with the improvements to the process. Other physicians across the country would eventually learn and adopt the techniques that the Denver group would develop. But most of us don't have ten years to wait for our local physicians to learn from the top experts. Realizing that there is such a huge difference in competence between practitioners in the medical community was a defining moment for me. I decided that never again would I assume that someone with MD beside their name knows as much as his or her peers. Going forward, I would look for the best medical practitioners that I could possibly find, using the best of my abilities and working within my resources. Sometimes it might mean re-prioritizing our lives to be able to apply additional resources to health care, but there was no doubt in my mind that it was the right thing to do.

After all, what is life without health? How can we be satis-
fied with our lives, knowing there is probably an answer to
our health problems out there? It would have cost us about
$20,000 to fail again using donor eggs in Cincinnati, com-
pared to about $28,000 (including travel costs) to try with
my own eggs in Denver. And what if we failed in Denver? At
least there would be the satisfaction of knowing we gave it
everything we had.

In June 2001, after an initial phone consultation with Dr. William
Schoolcraft, we made our first trip to the Colorado Center for
Reproductive Medicine in a suburb of Denver. This was a one-
day diagnostic and evaluation visit to help Dr. Schoolcraft and
his team get a full picture of what could be causing our infertility
issue. There were a number of tests conducted that were never
done in Cincinnati. This was our first indication that this place
did things differently and was potentially more thorough in their
assessment of individual patients' infertility causes. At the end
of the day, we had a conversation with Dr. Schoolcraft, who felt
that we were good candidates for in vitro fertilization under his
care at his clinic. I was encouraged, but could not let go of the
nagging question that had been brushed off by the Cincinnati
physician. So I asked Dr. Schoolcraft, "How do I know that an
embryo can implant in my uterus?" Dr. Schoolcraft's response
went something like this: "That's a very good question. Since you
brought it up, this is probably a good thing to look at based on
your history. There is a new test that looks for beta-3-integrins
in the lining of the uterus. These are little 'suction cup' proteins
that play an important role in the implantation of the embryo.
If they're not present, there is a treatment we can give you (one
injection per month for two months) that should clear things up
and allow the uterine lining to produce beta-3-integrins. There is
only one lab in the country that does this test and it costs $500."
WOW. Why wasn't this the answer I got in Cincinnati?

So my next step was to have a small piece of the uterine lining removed on a specific day of my cycle. A local physician in Cincinnati performed this procedure. The tissue sample was placed into a special container with instructions for shipment to the California laboratory for analysis. After waiting impatiently for a couple of weeks, I received a phone call from Dr. Schoolcraft's office reporting that my biopsy was negative for beta-3-integrins. I didn't have the suction cups! The follow up was to fill a prescription for leuprolide, which I was to self-inject on a specific day of my cycle for two cycles. Based on that timing, we could schedule the start of fertility medications in two months, followed by a ten-day trip to Denver beginning on September 26 to complete the in vitro fertilization cycle.

Now I was excited. I felt empowered. We were taking action, finding clues, and getting at the answers. I had high hopes that we would be parents soon. I did the injections, followed all the protocols exactly as instructed, started on the fertility medications, and was counting down the days to our trip to Denver.

Then came the horrific events of September 11, 2001. I remember vividly where I was and who I was with when I heard the radio announcements about the first airplane crashing into one of the World Trade Center towers. At first we assumed it was a terrible accident. Between this announcement and the rest of the news that would uncover several planes taken over in a terrorist attack, I was in a meeting with customers. As I got into my car after the meeting, I heard all the details about the second tower, the plane crash in Pennsylvania, and the plane hitting the Pentagon. I almost swerved off the road as I looked up into the sky and cringed in fear.

I had never experienced anything like this in my life. Rod had flown to Mexico early that morning. Was he okay? I had to reach him. No cellphone lines were operational. I received a call from my good friend Lisa, a colleague from the P&G Toronto office. She and a few others had flown in to Cincinnati from Toronto on a 7 a.m. Thank God! With Rod away, I really needed to hang out with someone I cared about that day. Lisa and I spent the rest of the afternoon and evening at my house, staring in disbelief and shedding tears at the images on the TV. As I'm sure is the case for most of you, it is difficult to describe the feelings we experienced that day and over the next several weeks. The closest I can come is to say it was a whole new depth of anger and sadness combined. I finally reached Rod that night and confirmed that he was okay. He was stranded in Mexico, since all flights into and out of the US were grounded for an unspecified number of days.

As I tried to get to sleep on that horrible night, I suddenly heard jets flying above my house. Since I knew that all flights were grounded, I started to panic. My heart was racing, as was my mind, imagining the worst possible scenarios. Then I remembered that we were not that far from the Dayton, Ohio, air-force base, and I realized these were probably air force jets patrolling the area. Since that night, I always feel a mild sense of panic when I hear airplanes over my house.

Over the next couple of days, Rod made his way home by driving a rental car to the Mexico–Texas border with his work colleagues and then renting the last car available in Laredo, Texas, to drive to Cincinnati. Lisa stayed at my house until commercial planes started flying again. With a deep sense of sadness in my heart, I started to have serious doubts about the wisdom of bringing a child into a world where humans could hate so much as to carry out such a horrific act. *Am I setting up a child for a future of fear and violence? Should I cancel my trip to Denver on September 26?*

Upon further reflection over the next two weeks, I came to the conclusion that we needed to carry on. We couldn't let the evil and negative forces in this world win. We would go forward with trying to build our family in defiance of the terrorists, and we would raise our kids to become powerful, positive forces in this world.

I left for Denver on September 26, 2001, and Rod followed a few days later. We stayed in a very low budget apartment-type rental unit with a lumpy bed, but it was functional and close to the fertility clinic. Since we did not have enough vacation days to cover the time away, both Rod and I received permission from our employers to work offsite from Denver for several days. For that, we were very grateful.

Between work and appointments at the clinic for blood tests, ultrasounds, etc., the days passed quickly. I discovered during our final pre-in vitro meeting with Dr. Schoolcraft that I had produced only four eggs. In my previous in vitro procedures, I had produced eight to ten. I asked if we should postpone and try again for another cycle, but Dr. Schoolcraft explained to me that this would not be a good choice. Not only does leuprolide reduce your ovaries' productivity, but the repeated use of injectable fertility medications can also reduce your success rate over time. I did not have the option of risking lower success rates, so we had to go ahead with this suboptimal number of eggs to choose from. On October 1, the egg retrieval took place, and the sperm was added to the eggs in a scientifically developed nutrient-rich medium. Then we crossed our fingers and hoped for high quality embryos on October 4, the planned embryo transfer day.

October 4 finally arrived, and we were greeted with the news that two of the embryos were of excellent quality and one was of good quality. The stars were aligned! So the three embryos were transferred into my uterus. During this entire process, we noted some significant differences between the Denver and Cincinnati procedures. To begin with, the Denver clinic had signs everywhere informing patients to refrain from wearing any perfume or deodorant in the egg retrieval and embryo transfer areas. We learned later that this is because eggs and embryos are very delicate, and their integrity can be compromised with the slightest environmental disturbance such as strong fumes. Also, there were no pictures taken of our embryos because it was believed even something like a flash could damage the embryos in some way. I was also instructed to remain on bed rest for forty-eight hours after the embryo transfer. I was curious why this was done, given what I was told by the Cincinnati physician, so I asked. Dr. Schoolcraft explained that we didn't want the body to divert blood flow to large muscles like the legs. We wanted to maximize the blood flow to the uterus to encourage a healthy implantation process. Now I understood! This made a lot of sense. I suppose the other doctor was right in stating that implantation was not a function of gravity, but she missed an important point about why the patient should stay off her feet.

Another difference between our experiences in Denver and Cincinnati was the treatment protocol to be followed after the embryo transfer. I don't remember the exact details, but there were more hormones to be injected with the Denver protocol, in an effort to optimize the preparation of the endometrium for implantation. We followed everything to the letter.

On October 18, 2001, I received the happiest news of my life up to that point. The voice at the other end of the phone said, "Congratulations, you're pregnant!" I can still picture myself at my desk in my home office on Old Village Drive in Loveland, a suburb of Cincinnati. My heart jumped. I thought I would explode with excitement. I called Rod the second I hung up the phone with the nurse in Denver. I was crying with joy. We were both so happy, relieved, and gratified that our perseverance had paid off. My next call was to my parents. My mom answered, and I immediately said, "Mom, get Dad on the phone!" As soon as he came on I said, "Are you ready to be grandparents?" They were overjoyed for us.

After this wonderful experience and the birth of our beautiful baby girl, Arquelle, in June 2002, there was no doubt in our minds that we were going back to Denver for our second baby, assuming we could not get pregnant on our own over the next six months or so. It sounds crazy to be trying to get pregnant so soon after having the first, but I was thirty-six. The clock was ticking, particularly with my history of infertility. Every month counted. About nine months after Arquelle was born, we were beginning the process of in vitro fertilization again and headed to Denver in April 2003. The embryo transfer occurred on April 25, our eleventh wedding anniversary. We felt confident about it, despite the fact that blood tests had revealed my odds of getting pregnant had dropped by 50 per cent since June 2001. Specific hormone levels were indicating the approach of menopause at an earlier-than-average age, and I was quickly running out of time. This attempt had to be successful.

Once again, we were very diligent in following instructions, and the reward was a positive pregnancy test on May 9, 2003. Our second "miracle baby" Sabrina was born in January 2004.

Interestingly, my two pregnancies seemed to provide some relief to the generalized muscle stiffness. Additionally, I had noticed that I usually felt worse during the week before my period and got some relief the day my period started. These facts should have provided additional clues as to the systemic nature of my problem. In my opinion, it is likely that the hormonal changes associated with pregnancy and the menstrual cycle had an impact on the soft tissues. Had I been a fully-fledged health champion at the time, I would have put those clues together and discussed them with conviction with a health professional who was willing to listen and help solve the problem with me.

Chapter 4—Looking Back: Lessons Learned

✓ If you don't like what you're hearing from one health professional, keep asking questions and searching for other opinions and expertise. Not all health professionals are created equal.

✓ Use your social network. If people don't know that you're struggling with a health issue, they can't help you. Be selective, but don't be afraid to share your challenges with friends, colleagues, and family members. You'd be surprised where this can lead.

✓ Follow all leads offered to you. You don't know what you don't know. If something doesn't really make sense, check it out anyway. You can always rule it out later.

✓ If you have access to top experts in the field, insist on seeing them early in the process. This means you have to work on identifying the experts and convincing the "gatekeepers" that you need to see the experts. In Canada, the gatekeepers are usually the general practitioners or family physicians.

✓ If there are costs involved, think of the value of a successful outcome with the more experienced and proven professional, compared to the frustration of repeated failures with lower cost options. In what areas could you reduce spending in order to build your "health and wellness fund?"

✓ No matter how great the reputation of the health professional, ask all questions that come to mind. The more you know about your symptoms or condition, the better your questions. But there are no bad questions. You'd be amazed at how you can trigger the professional to consider different aspects of your problem. Imagine if I hadn't asked Dr. Schoolcraft about whether the embryos could implant in my uterus.

Chapter 4—Health Champion in Action

Losing Vision and Protecting What was Left

Many missed clues on the part of both my mom and her health professionals led to her losing most of the vision in one eye to macular degeneration. The good news is that once this was identified and diagnosed, she was referred to a very knowledgeable ophthalmologist who provided her with the treatments needed to preserve what little sight she had remaining in the damaged eye. More importantly, having him as a resource was important in protecting the vision in her good eye. After doing some of my own research on macular degeneration, I asked to come along on one of her follow-up visits with this specialist. My goal was to make sure my mom had all the information and guidance necessary to prevent the loss of vision in her good eye.

During the doctor's visit, I could tell he was an expert in his field by the way he answered my questions directly and without hesitation or condescension. One of my questions pertained to the usefulness of low dose Aspirin in reducing the risk of macular degeneration, which had come up in my research. He responded that the data was not supportive of this, however, he did add: "Oh, yes, that reminds me. Your mom should make sure she takes omega-3 supplements since there is some good evidence that those are protective to the eyes."

The lesson in this case is that asking a question, any question, can lead to more solutions. There are no bad questions if you are dealing with a knowledgeable health professional. It's about initiating a dialogue that can trigger further problem solving by your health professional. You are ultimately responsible for solving your health problems; health professionals are just one of your resources on this problem-solving journey.

5

THE UPS AND DOWNS

In 1998, after our move to Cincinnati, I began to explore the US health care system. I was dealing not only with the chronic pain and stiffness on the left side of my body, but also with all of the injuries that occurred as I tried to remain as physically active as I could.

I started out looking for help from a sports medicine clinic, which I later realized was mainly populated with orthopedic surgeons. One of the many things I learned through my ordeal is that orthopedic surgeons can be helpful as long as you have a diagnosed mechanical problem that can be repaired through surgery. Unfortunately, this was not the case for me. One of the treatments the surgeon offered for my chronic left hip problem was a cortisone injection into the sacroiliac joint, under x-ray visualization. This seemed to offer some relief. Again, this offered another clue to the problem: if cortisone helped, there was inflammation involved. If I had only known that there would be no single answer, I would have begun putting all the clues together and implementing all the potential solutions at once. I did clue in to the anti-inflammatory concept and began taking non-steroidal anti-inflammatory drugs (such as ibuprofen and naproxen) on and off over the next several years. Most of the time they did provide some temporary relief, until they caused a gastrointestinal bleed in 2007. But there was so much more required to get to the level I wanted to reach...and no one to point this out to me for so many years.

The injuries continued to pile up, at first mainly when doing strenuous things like playing tennis or running, but over time I would pull something simply by making a sudden movement like turning my head too fast. My neck became really stiff and something as simple as tilting my head to kiss Rod became a major challenge. Each time I had a new soft tissue injury, it was treated as a "one-off." Not once between 1996 and 2009 did someone suggest that there could be an underlying condition driving the continued stiffness and injury proneness.

Around 1999 or 2000, when I saw yet another doctor about my chronic pain and stiffness, I was again referred to a physiotherapist. I was pretty skeptical, since I had worked with physiotherapists before and had limited success. Right away, Barbara struck me as different in her approach. She did a complete assessment and recommended all types of exercises designed to improve my range of motion from neck to ankles. I had been talking to her mainly about the hip area, so I thought it was strange that she was showing me stuff for the upper body too. At the time, the stiffness had gotten really bad, and I had such limited range of motion that I found some of these basic exercises challenging. Once again, I wasn't convinced that discomfort was part of the process for getting better, and I implemented the exercises irregularly at best. I did notice, however, that I seemed to feel better after doing some of her prescribed exercises. But not being convinced of their value, I let life take over and gradually stopped doing most of them, except some rolling and stretching (the short-term relief stuff).

One day in 2003, I developed symptoms I had never felt before, which included numbness and tingling down my leg into my foot. I saw an orthopedic surgeon who ordered an MRI that revealed a herniated disc in my lower back. Here was my opportunity to blame everything on a concrete, visually detected problem! *This must be it,* I thought. *This herniated disc must be the source of all my misery for these past eight years!* When the orthopedic surgeon didn't agree that all of my other chronic symptoms could be linked to this disc issue, I decided to get a second opinion from another orthopedic surgeon who specialized in spines. His opinion was the same. All of the chronic muscle stiffness I was describing was not likely due to this herniated disc. The more recent pain and numbness in the hips and legs could be explained by it, but not all the other older symptoms. So he offered to send me to a physiotherapist (again) to try to address the soft tissue problems I was describing. It couldn't hurt since physiotherapy could also help with the disc issue. I agreed to return to Barbara.

Again, I was intrigued by Barbara's approach. It was very different. As I learned later, she was exploring active release and trying to release myofascial adhesions and trigger points—areas where the muscle and connective tissue are bunched up, stuck together, or in knots. She started with studying my posture very closely and noticed that I was, as she called it, "crooked." My right shoulder was down and forward and my left hip was rotated forward. I began to realize that most of the injuries I was experiencing—tears in the calf muscle, several "pulls" of various muscles along both sides of my body, Achilles tendinitis, shoulder tendinitis, patellar (front of the knee) tendinitis, and, most recently, this herniated disc—were due to the left-right imbalance in my body caused by my left side being "locked up." She gave me some instruction on how to get my body reprogrammed into as symmetrical a position as possible. She had me consciously move shoulders and hips into positions that were more balanced. Just by doing this, I was feeling some relief. She also introduced the foam roller and a specialty "massage ball" to help release trigger points and adhesions that were all over my body. I had already discovered rolling on a tennis ball, but the systematic rolling with a roller and a massage ball designed to press into the tissue like a human thumb was new to me. Barbara gave me yet more exercises to do. Some were the same as before, others were new. Most of them were designed to build strength while releasing the fascia (connective tissue) and lengthening the muscles. There was definitely some sporadic improvement while I saw her.

From January 2004 to the beginning of 2005 was a difficult period for me, as I suffered from postpartum depression after the birth of my second daughter. Although it was never diagnosed, I now know what it was. It was particularly bad after I returned to work in June 2004 and stress levels mounted with demands on me both at work and at home. Rod was travelling internationally for extended periods and I had no family support network in Cincinnati. I had friends, but not the kind of close friends you felt comfortable calling and asking for help. I felt a sense of helplessness combined with exhaustion and chronic stress. Tears and meltdowns occurred at the drop of a hat. I did mention it to my family doctor at one point who was ready to prescribe antidepressants. I said no thanks.

Then July 10, 2005, happened. Just as I was pulling out of my depression and starting to regain a sense of mental wellbeing, my parents were in a car accident and my dad was killed.

I didn't feel anything for the next six months. It took a long time to be able to smile again. I was determined to find a lesson from my dad's death; I decided to focus on cherishing every moment I had with my beautiful children. I realized that this life is temporary and that each day could be the last with them. Through the deep sadness, I thanked my dad for the gift of appreciating every moment of my life. I was thankful for the fact that he lived to meet his grandchildren and tried not to focus on how much it hurt that he couldn't see them grow up. Time didn't necessarily heal the pain and sadness of this greatest loss of my life, but it certainly allowed me to coexist with them.

While in a session with my massage therapist in 2006, she suggested, as she had previously, that I might benefit from seeing a "Rolfer." She explained the Rolfing technique as a type of massage therapy that was focused on structural issues and would go deeper than what she could do (which was pretty deep and painful at times). The name comes from Dr. Ida Rolf, who developed the technique, also called structural integration, in the mid-twentieth century. Given Barbara's comments about my "crookedness" and knowing that postural shifts did make a difference on how I felt, I thought it would be a good idea to try this Rolfing thing. My massage therapist had learned of a good practitioner from one of her clients, so she gave me his contact information.

James the Rolfer (or structural integrationist as he should be appropriately called) was an interesting person. As I walked into his studio, it struck me as a bit odd. There was a large mattress on the floor with a five or six foot high wooden frame surrounding it. James was a slight man, very soft spoken. The first session consisted mainly of him observing my standing and walking while taking pictures and notes. We then began our sessions where he would work on my body in an effort to release and align the soft tissues to allow better functioning. I learned over the next several weeks that James had been in a serious bicycle accident and had studied the Rolf Method of Structural Integration in an effort to "fix himself." I could tell he believed in his work and really wanted to help others. After only a few sessions I was feeling some significant improvements in terms of reduced stiffness.

Then one day, I woke up with a really bad pain in my right shoulder. It was as if the relief of all the surrounding stiffness that I had achieved through Rolfing had revealed a shoulder problem. As I discovered later, this is how my body works. Inflammation in one area begets widespread stiffness and muscle contraction. The stiffness then puts me at risk for other injuries that result in inflammation, and the cycle starts again.

I brought my shoulder pain complaint to the orthopedic surgeon. He confirmed via MRI that I had tendinitis in my rotator cuff, at the front of my shoulder. He suggested we start with physical therapy to see how much improvement could be gained, but said that if I wanted to continue playing tennis regularly, it was likely I would require surgery to free the tendon that was being impinged by a bone. After a few weeks of diligently following the stretching and strengthening exercises prescribed by the physiotherapist, I did start to feel quite a bit better. And not just in my shoulder. Strangely, I was feeling relief from stiffness right down into my hips. All the while, I continued to see James the Rolfer, whose work I'm sure continued to help with improvements all across my body.

During a Florida vacation around this time, I was feeling well enough to attempt one of my rare runs. As I started my warm-up and stretching routine, I put my leg up on a bar in the gym to do a hamstring stretch. Just as I realized the bar was a little too high, I lost my balance. I tried to catch myself by pivoting on the foot that was planted on the floor, but the floor was covered with a non-slip rubber surface. So instead of my foot pivoting, it was my knee that twisted. I felt and heard a "snap" as I went down in pain, beating myself up mentally for being such an idiot. *Just as I'm starting to feel really good! Why can't I be a normal person who would just choose to go and lie by the pool and revel in the fact that my body was feeling less stiff and sore? Oh no, not me. I have to try and go for a run the minute there's any sign of improvement in my condition.* But then I realized: that's me, isn't it? That's why I'm so annoyed and irritated at this condition of mine. It's because I'm not free to move how and when I want to. My knee swelled up like a balloon and I was forced to lie around for the remainder of the vacation, thinking about the wasted opportunity for increased physical activity during this window of improved physical functioning. A visit to my orthopedic surgeon upon our return home indicated that I had simply overextended a ligament, and no serious damage was done.

I was convinced that I needed the shoulder surgery in order to continue playing tennis. Right around this time (early 2007), Rod was offered a work transfer back to the Toronto area. Although this was welcome news for us, we knew that my shoulder surgery would be considered a low priority within the Canadian medical system, and that I would have to wait a long time for the surgery once in Canada. I took advantage of having a good medical plan in Cincinnati and was able to schedule the surgery within three weeks of making the decision to go ahead with it. Having two young children ages three and four and Rod already working in Toronto, I must admit it was challenging to go through with the surgery.

The first week after surgery involved a lot of pain. Two weeks later I got on a plane from Cincinnati to Toronto, alone with two little kids and lots of luggage. I vowed to continue with my physiotherapy exercises every day and get that shoulder to 100 per cent as soon as I could. As I continued with the recovery and the exercises, my entire body felt better. I shared this with my surgeon in a follow up appointment, and he laughed at me. He did not believe that relief of the inflammation and strengthening of the muscles in the shoulder area could relieve tightness and discomfort that was occurring along the connective tissue in my body. Much later, I would learn about how few medical experts are knowledgeable about conditions related to soft tissue and the myofascial "chains" that exist in the body.

Throughout 2007, with continued determination to do my shoulder exercises almost every day, I saw significant improvements in my condition. I was convinced I was "cured." I started running again (short distances), continued working on my upper body strength, and increased the frequency and fervor with which I played tennis. I was also settling back into the Toronto office at P&G Pharmaceuticals. After being away for nine years, one of the highlights was spending time with my good friend Lisa once again.

Lisa convinced me to join a Masters Swimming program with her in late 2008. I hated swimming because I wasn't very good at it. In my first class, I could hardly complete one lap of front crawl without desperately gasping for air. With a few tips from the instructor over the next several classes, I began to understand how I could swim more efficiently and be less tired after each lap. These glimmers of hope that my stroke could improve kept me going back.

Lisa started talking about doing a triathlon in August 2009. Since I was feeling pretty good (at least better than the last twelve years), I thought that would be a great challenge. We targeted the sprint distance race at the Subaru Triathlon Series event in Niagara. This would involve a 750 m swim in Lake Ontario, a 25 km bike ride, and a 7 km run. I had never done an open water swim in my life. This appeared like a giant challenge at the time, but I wanted to try *something*, since I was feeling so much better than I had in years. A marathon, or even a half-marathon, was out of the question in my mind, but at least I could prove to myself I could do something physically challenging. And the cross-training would be easier on my body. Although Lisa changed her mind about participating in the triathlon, I continued to pursue the goal.

Until May of 2009, training had been going well. I was starting to think I could be physically active without being chronically injured. My swimming was improving, though I was still the slowest in the slow lane at the Masters Swimming program. One day, I felt like I pulled something in my left lat muscle, the muscle that sits at the side of the body, below the armpit. Gradually, it started to tighten up and cause problems all around the shoulder, back, and chest area. I had to take a break from swimming and stopped playing tennis. But I could still run and bike, so the triathlon still seemed possible. Three weeks later, I pulled something in my left calf. Based on my past experience, it was no coincidence that this was on the same side as my lat/shoulder injury. Now I couldn't run, but I could do the elliptical trainer and the bike. So I focused on those two and still believed I might be able to recover in time for the August race. Over the next couple of months, a familiar process started to happen. It seemed like whenever I did a motion that required some force from my left side (e.g., sweeping the concrete in the backyard), I would irritate my shoulder and would feel pain and tightness all down my left side. By early July (four or five weeks before the race), I was seriously questioning whether I could do this triathlon. After all, I had not been swimming since May and had not run since June. I was nowhere close to being able to swim 750 m without stopping and run 7 km after swimming and biking. The only thing I was pretty confident about was the bike.

After having seen a glimmer of hope in 2008 and early 2009, these emerging issues were devastating. I had turned to doctors and chiropractors to get help, and nothing seemed to work. The frustration, helplessness, and anger were even stronger than they had been during the previous twelve years.

Chapter 5—Looking Back: Lessons Learned

✓ If a particular approach gives you partial or temporary relief, pursue it like a dog with a bone. Understand WHY it is helping, and ask as many health professionals as possible about what other types of related approaches might also help. If you understand the logic behind it, you might be more motivated to persevere with it for a while.

✓ Don't drop one approach in favor of another that you think might work better. Add the new approach to the others if at all possible. There's a good chance the benefits will be cumulative.

✓ Recognize that different health professionals have different answers. You cannot assume that the health professional sitting in front of you at any particular moment is the one who can best help you with your current problem.

✓ Listen closely to each health professional's point of view and pay attention to the things that provide even minor relief. These are all clues that YOU are responsible for putting together to arrive at the overall solution.

✓ Pay particular attention if two or more health professionals are giving you similar advice. Keep digging for information along those lines. The more you can confirm for yourself that you're headed down the right path, the more likely you are to take action towards the recommended treatments, exercises, etc.

✓ Pay attention to what is happening in your body, and add any recognizable symptom patterns to your list of clues to be researched or discussed with trusted health professionals.

Chapter 5—Health Champion in Action

The Sore Toe Story

On this particular occasion, my mom had dropped the corner of a couch on her toe while cleaning the house. The pain was pretty intense, so she decided to go to the hospital. Despite her telling the ER staff about the couch accident, the attending physician decided there was a good possibility that she had gout and ordered blood tests to rule out gout as a cause for the inflamed toe. Of course the blood test came back negative for gout.

In this case, the doctor saw an inflamed toe on an elderly woman, and, based on a standard algorithm, recognized that it could signal gout. But he chose to ignore a key part of solving this problem, which was the patient's description of how the toe became inflamed! This doctor was a protocol-follower and not a problem solver.

Health Champions need to be on the lookout for these types of interactions with health care professionals. When your description of the situation is not properly taken into account by the doctor or other professional, it might be a sign that you need to look for another health professional, particularly if this is a recurring problem in your interactions with a particular health professional.

THE BREAKTHROUGH

Just as I was struggling with the very real possibility that I would not be able to participate in this sprint triathlon for which I had been training, my best friend, MT, tore a ligament in her foot and discovered a multidisciplinary sports medicine clinic that seemed to do things differently. It was the Institute for Sports Medicine (ISM), the clinic led by Dr. Anthony Galea, which included professional and Olympic athletes on its client list. On MT's recommendation, I talked to some of the therapists to see if they had any suggestions for me. One of them pointed me to Jillian Halligan, an Exercise Physiologist and strength coach affiliated with the clinic. Three weeks before the race, I had my first appointment with her. Little did I know she would change my life.

When I told Jillian my story, she immediately concluded that there must be something biochemical or systemic causing my issues. Knowing I really wanted to do this triathlon in three weeks, she advised me to start taking magnesium and omega-3 supplements. She also instructed me to do some ice massage on my problem areas, mainly my shoulder at this point. We agreed I shouldn't start a new exercise program right before the race. The goal was to show up and finish the race, and then Jill would work with me to get to a better place. She had confidence that I could improve a lot, but I would need to commit to following her program to the letter, and I would likely need to get some blood tests done to understand what my systemic issues were.

The chiropractor I had been seeing with limited success at the time was going on vacation the week before my race. His advice was for me to book a sports massage with the best massage therapist at his clinic for the day before the race. That was the best thing he did for me. Tonya was amazing. In addition to her incredible massage, she recommended an Epsom salt bath and lots of hydration that night, which I did. When I went to bed, I was scared. Part of me was determined to do the race, and part of me wanted to just forget about it, since I was injured and not properly trained. Something happened that night that was truly mind-boggling. I was lying in bed, butterflies in my stomach, thinking about the next morning when I felt a gentle squeeze on my left thigh. It was the kind of squeeze that a good friend would give you to say, "Don't worry. Everything will be okay. You'll do great." Rod was asleep to my right and there was no one else in the room! I'm convinced it was my dad there with me.

I really don't know what made me get up at 5 a.m. that day and go alone to do a triathlon for which I was not fully trained. What I did know was that for a few months in the past year or two, I appeared to be making significant progress, likely due to the post-surgery shoulder exercises. Although I didn't understand it at the time, those exercises were the right movements to break up myofascial and scar tissue and strengthen weak muscles. That morning, something inside me thought: *I have to seize this opportunity...this could be the closest I'll ever come to being ready for a triathlon. Yes, everything is stiff and sore, but let's just see what I can do.* In fact, when I woke up that morning my body felt better than it had felt the past several weeks. It certainly didn't hurt that I had an incredibly positive and supportive husband who never once questioned my decision to go for it, despite being injured and unable to swim or run for the last several months! Not only did he encourage me, but he got our seven- and five-year-old kids up at 6:30 that morning so that the family could come and cheer for me. My brother and his wife also gave up their day to come and encourage me.

I was incredibly nervous driving myself to the race. (Rod and the kids were about 90 minutes behind me.) But there is an indescribable power in believing this could be your only chance to do something physically challenging that you never thought you could even come close to. In my mind, this was *it*. If I could just finish this race, I would be satisfied, knowing I pushed myself to the limit. In fact, I had three very clear goals for this race:

1. Don't develop any new injuries or worsen existing injuries;

2. Finish the race;

3. Don't be last in your age group (which at that point wouldn't have mattered as long as #1 and #2 were achieved).

Walking from the parking lot to the race site was intimidating, with lots of people looking like "real" triathletes. There I was with my $700 hybrid bike surrounded by expensive racing bikes. I had read all the pre-race instructions carefully, so I got my bike on the rack in the right place and went to the various stations to receive my race number, swim cap, and body markings.

This was my first time putting on a wetsuit. I had rented one from a triathlon shop in Toronto after deciding at the last minute that it might be a good idea. As it turned out, the wetsuit was one of the key factors that allowed me to get through the swim. Lake Ontario was 70 degrees F. For perspective, I don't swim in my pool if it's less than 87 degrees F! I put on the wetsuit backwards and then realized the zipper goes in the back.

As the start time approached, I placed myself in the rear outside corner of the swim pack. This huge body of water scared me to death; it looked really dark and the waves were significant, thanks to the unsettled weather. The buoys were arranged in such a way that I would have to round three corners before heading back into shore. The first buoy looked impossibly far away. My heart rate was over 120 beats per minute before even starting the swim.

Before the start gun, I spotted Rod and the kids on shore, as well as my brother Mike and his wife, Kerry. Boy was I glad to see them. The start gun went off, and I started to swim front crawl. This lasted about 50 m (about two minutes) then I had to turn on my back. I started to panic and told myself that there was no way I could get through this swim. I did a few strokes of the elementary backstroke ("frog kick"). I was about to put my hand up to be rescued by a lifeguard, which would have ended my race. Knowing that Rod and the kids were watching, however, made me think I should give it a harder try. So I went back to doing the front crawl for about 25 m or less at a time, alternating onto my back for 25–50 meters. Before I knew it, I was pretty close to making the turn at the first buoy, and the next stretch to the second buoy was quite a bit shorter than the distance I had just completed. *Okay, so maybe I can make it to the second turn.* Continuing with mainly breaststroke and elementary backstroke, I somehow made it to the second turn. By this point, I thought again about raising my hand to be rescued, and I could see one of the lifeguards looking at me with concern. Once again, I thought about Rod and the kids, my brother and his wife. *If I can just get through this part, then I know I can do the bike and the run (or walk).* Looking ahead, it was one more long stretch followed by a slight turn at the last buoy, and I could see my way to the shore! *Okay, I have to do this. I don't care if it's elementary backstroke all the way.* People from the next start group were passing me. When I finally made it out of the water, I felt dizzy and disoriented, but ecstatic! I did it! I got out!

When I got to the transition area, I tried to remove my wetsuit. I don't know if it was shock, exhaustion, or cold (probably a combination), but my arms and hands had no strength at all, and I could not even begin to pull off the wetsuit! So I waited a few minutes and tried again. I kept working at it until my strength came back, and I was finally able to pull it off. Then I felt a sense of total freedom. *I did it! I made it in before the swim cut-off time, pulled the wetsuit off, and now I know I can finish this race.*

For the first half of the bike ride, I was so happy that I really didn't pay attention to the fact that it was a race and not a little jaunt through the park. I sort of woke up with about 10 km left and tried to go a little faster. After the bike, I took a few minutes in transition to stretch and improve my chances of running rather than walking the 7 km. To my surprise, I ended up running almost all of it. When I hit the 6 km mark I thought to myself: *This is never going to end, so just accept the suffering and shut your brain off.* I entered a sort of cruise control, which can also be called "the zone." I wasn't even looking for the finish line when I rounded a corner and there it was! There were my husband, kids, brother, and sister-in-law all cheering for me! It's very difficult to explain the emotions as I crossed that finish line. Exhilaration comes to mind. Gratitude, relief, and pride also come to mind. I started crying, gasped for air and hugged my support crew. Two hours and 24 minutes. Monumental!

When it was all over, my five-year-old daughter asked me "Did you win, Mommy?" I paused for a second and answered, "Yes, sweetie. I won *my* race." This was truly the greatest victory of my life to this point. It was my breakthrough moment. One of the most powerful drivers that made me show up that morning was the thought that, given that my body was beginning to fail again, this could realistically be my only opportunity to participate in a triathlon. I now truly understood the meaning of having a "stretch goal," something you're not really sure how you can accomplish, but you surrender to that little glimmer of hope in your mind and to the voice that says, "Just maybe I can." What if we looked at all stretch goals that way? Life is so unpredictable that any undertaking could be our last for whatever reason.

After this huge accomplishment, I was on top of the world and ready to start working with Jillian. I wanted to know if I could get to a point where I could train for something like this again, without all the injuries piling up along the way. I imagined what it could be like if I were fully trained and injury-free before doing a race like this. Rod became so wrapped up in the excitement of the race and my exhilaration that he decided to participate in this same triathlon with me the following year. How great would that be?

Interestingly, my muscles actually felt better after the race than they did before. Yes, there was some of that "good" soreness that one feels after a workout, but much less of the "bad" stiffness and soreness I had been used to for the last thirteen years. Somewhat encouraged and optimistic, I started working with Jillian. This was an incredible discovery process. She conducted her initial assessment, which revealed a number of weaknesses and imbalances across my body. Not only was I weak in many areas, but my range of motion and flexibility were very limited as well. For the first several months, my program consisted mainly of range of motion, flexibility, and balance exercises that I did on my own in between sessions. Every three to four weeks she would add on a new aspect to the training program. One of the things that was different about working with Jillian was that she explained why it was important to stick with every exercise she gave me, unlike the physiotherapists I had worked with in the past. And not only was it important to do all the exercises, it was important to do them in the order in which she wrote them into my program. She was so knowledgeable and confident about how and why these exercises would help, that it made me believe. I'm not sure I would have been convinced to follow through with certain moves if anyone else had directed me to do them.

By the time I had been working with Jillian for four months, I was making significant progress related to range of motion and I was having more and more good days with fewer symptoms overall. She was beginning to introduce more strength-building exercises, which often felt uncomfortable or even scary given my history of chronic injuries. As the program became more challenging, I started to revert to my thinking that if a particular exercise didn't feel good, I should avoid it. When doing the program by myself, I would skip a few of the more difficult and uncomfortable moves. One in particular was the lateral squat walk, which consisted of walking side to side in a squat position with a thick rubber band around your ankles. By this point, Rod had also signed up with Jillian after seeing how much she was helping me. He also had the lateral squat walks on his program. As we were working out together one day, he said, "Those #@#** squat walks are so hard. I hate them." I totally agreed with him, briefly feeling justified in skipping the move. Then he surprised me with: "I guess that's why we need to do them!" *Wow,* I thought to myself. *How stupid have I been? Of course! They are unpleasant and uncomfortable because I am weak in the outer hips. This is why I need this specific exercise!* This was a huge wake-up moment for me. It seems so obvious now, but if I had continued thinking I knew better, I'm pretty sure I would not be where I am today.

There was also the time when my knee swelled up for no apparent reason, and I thought to myself: *Here we go again. It must be one of the exercises that is just too much for me. I'll bet it's those one-legged squats. I have to stop doing those.* When I showed Jillian my knee and told her I was pretty sure it was caused by one-legged squats (which also happened to be difficult and uncomfortable), she reassured me that she was not showing me any moves that could cause damage to my body. Her advice was to keep doing the squats, but only to the point where they didn't hurt. Even if I could only go down an inch, that was fine. She also looked at my form to make sure I was aligning my knee properly over my foot when doing the squat. I must admit that I was a bit disappointed when she insisted that I needed to continue doing these exercises in order to build the strength to avoid future injuries. There was a pattern developing here. The more I hated the move, the more I needed to do it. But just the thought of being able to do another triathlon with a better result than last time kept me going and I pushed through the discomfort. Another key motivator was the fact that Rod was also training to do this triathlon with me.

In addition to this progressive strength-training program, Jillian advised that I get a very comprehensive blood analysis done, in consultation with Dr. Galea. The blood test results combined with my symptom history were shared with a Ph.D. biochemist specializing in nutritional science, who used the information to develop a nutrition program tailored to my needs. Some of the key findings from my blood work included a low magnesium level and indications that there was something strange happening with my levels of insulin, the hormone that causes the body's various tissues to absorb glucose from the blood and use it for energy or storage. The analysis of the food diary I had been asked to keep over the last week indicated consumption of a lot of processed carbohydrates and relatively low levels of protein and greens.

My **nutrition and supplement plan** included the following key principles to ensure my muscles and connective tissues could operate at their full potential:

✓ Increase protein intake by almost doubling my current intake. Meat sources should be organic.

✓ Reduce or eliminate processed sugar.

✓ Select only unprocessed carbohydrates.

✓ Dramatically increase my intake of omega fatty acids, which meant eating a lot of fish (something I wasn't particularly fond of), raw seeds, and avocados and taking an omega-3 supplement.

✓ Increase magnesium intake by eating lots of green leafy vegetables and taking daily supplements (ensuring that magnesium is accompanied with calcium—about 2:1 magnesium to calcium ratio).

Another helpful tool introduced to me by Jillian was Frequency Specific Microcurrent or FSM. Although electromagnetic principles in medicine date back as far as the late 1800s, modern use of electrical frequencies in healing was spearheaded in the 1940s by Harry Van Gelder, a naturopath and osteopath in Vancouver, BC. In the late 1990s, the clinical use of very low-level electrical currents set at varying frequencies became known as Frequency Specific Microcurrent or FSM and its use began to spread through the chiropractor and physician communities throughout North America. FSM offers treatment options (protocols) for a broad range of medical conditions, including inflammation in muscle and connective tissues. I went for several FSM sessions at ISM and also borrowed Jillian's portable machine for a week. I could tell this was making a difference. Since it was too inconvenient for me to go to the clinic three times per week, I decided to invest in my own portable FSM machine. I use it quite regularly to this day, under the guidance of an osteopathic practitioner, for dealing with both old and new soft tissue problems. It has also been quite useful for family members when musculoskeletal or other problems arise for which there is a protocol on the FSM machine.

Chapter 6—Looking Back: Lessons Learned

✓ Until you have met a true problem solver like Jillian, you have not gone as far as you can in your search for help with your condition. There is the possibility that it will not be an MD who provides the breakthrough clues that lead to solving your problem. If it is an MD who holds the keys, there is a good chance it won't be the first one you see. Keep searching.

✓ If it doesn't feel good or you "can't" do something, it's probably because you don't have the strength to do it...yet. That's why you need to keep working on it!

✓ As long as you're working with someone who you believe is competent in his or her field, be sure to think twice before making your own judgments about whether certain treatments or exercises are good for you or not. Ask your health professional for a rationale as to why you should continue doing something that doesn't feel good to you. Getting a satisfactory answer to this question could save you years of pain and distress if it compels you to implement something that ultimately works.

✓ If possible, drag a friend into your goal or challenge. Better yet, find a friend, colleague, or family member who has a similar goal. They will likely motivate you to push a little harder.

✓ I can't emphasize enough how you need to establish your *why* for your goal. When things get difficult and you feel like giving up, go back to that why. Picture yourself achieving the goal and let yourself feel the positive emotions that will come to you at that moment.

✓ No matter what type of health professional you're working with, explore questions around nutritional requirements and blood analysis to determine whether there is a deficiency in elements important to addressing your problem. For most of my twenties and early thirties, I was a vegetarian who didn't like fish, eggs or vegetables. In addition, I had lactose intolerance and avoided most dairy products. How much protein and other nutrients critical to muscle and connective tissue function do you think I was taking in on a daily basis? Not even close to sufficient quantities would be my guess. Not one doctor asked me any details about my diet. If you don't bring it up, they likely won't ask.

Chapter 6—Health Champion in Action

The Frustrating Back Problem

When I recently asked a group of highly educated and motivated women about health issues they've overcome by taking on the health champion role, Tina spoke up about her experience with a back problem a few years earlier. She was having chronic pain in her lower back and had been to the doctor several times only to be sent home with a prescription for anti-inflammatories. After a few months of frustration, she decided to buy a book about how to deal with back pain and implemented the recommended exercises religiously. Within a matter of a few months, she was free of the back problem. The book helped her understand why the exercises were important, which motivated her to implement them.

7

BUILDING CONFIDENCE

From 2010 to 2013, my strength and physical abilities continued to increase along with the belief that my life had changed forever. I was so thrilled with this new sense of relief from chronic pain and stiffness that I felt the need to keep trying more and more challenging distances of triathlon. My body was not perfect and probably never will be, but I did what I could to be the best I could be. I was incredibly diligent with my new nutrition and supplement plan, strength-training program, regular yoga classes, and chiropractic visits.

On days when I felt stiffer than usual, I would sometimes take to researching what this condition could be and what else I could do to reduce the symptoms. Despite all of my progress, I still didn't have a label for it. One day I came across an interesting article about fibromyalgia and the types of underlying issues that were associated with its symptoms, which were similar to mine, though not identical. There were several issues related to fibromyalgia that caught my attention. I found myself nodding my head as I read through the list of symptoms:

- ✪ Low levels of magnesium
- ✪ A lot of growing pains as a child
- ✪ "Rebound hypoglycemia"—low blood sugar a few hours after eating
- ✪ Susceptibility to stomach irritation
- ✪ Lack of good quality sleep

For the past five years, my husband told me that I snored a lot and actually woke myself up frequently throughout the night. After pondering the lack of quality sleep and its potential role in fibromyalgia, I decided to bring up the snoring problem with my family doctor who referred me to a sleep specialist. This doctor really knew his data regarding sleep apnea, a condition in which the patient stops breathing in the middle of the night. He answered all my questions confidently, quoted the literature, and appreciated the fact that I had done my research in advance. I respected his opinion. His recommendation was a sleep study in which they would evaluate whether or not my snoring was related to apnea and if so, how serious the apnea was. To my surprise, the sleep study revealed that I stopped breathing over 150 times during the night, indicating that I had moderate to severe sleep apnea. I also learned that, if left untreated, sleep apnea is associated with a much higher risk of heart disease and a shortened life expectancy. Could this be yet another piece of the puzzle related to my myofascial symptoms? Whether it was or not, I needed to deal with this apnea.

The sleep specialist informed me that the most effective treatment for sleep apnea is a CPAP (Continuous Positive Airway Pressure) machine. It is 95 per cent effective in reducing apnea episodes. This sounded great. Where do I sign up? As I sat with the CPAP consultant, my heart sank. In fact, I felt a lump in my throat and almost started crying. They expected me to wear what looked like an oxygen mask attached to a tube leading to a machine that would force air into my mouth and nose. It sounded like Darth Vader was in the room. After almost twenty years of marriage, I wasn't overly concerned about looking unsexy to my husband, but still...I had a little bit of vanity left in me. I had to go away and think about it. When Rod and I talked about it, his opinion was that I needed to get the machine because of the long-term health risks of untreated sleep apnea. I knew he was right, and I reluctantly took my CPAP machine home the following week.

It was a mental, emotional, and physical struggle to try to keep the mask on every night. I could not figure out how anyone could use this machine every night for the rest of their lives. Not only did I feel confined and claustrophobic when putting the mask on, making it difficult to get to sleep, but I would also unconsciously remove the mask in the middle of the night. I wasn't sure how many hours I actually wore it. Apparently, there isn't much benefit in wearing the mask for less than five hours. According to some reports, between 60 and 90 per cent of CPAP users stopped using their machines by the end of the first year. This was no surprise to me, given my experience so far. What good is 95 per cent efficacy if you don't actually use the treatment?

After struggling with the CPAP machine for about three months, I started to search for an alternative. I consulted with a lot of people including health professionals and did some internet searches. Finally I came upon a solution that might work: a custom molded dental appliance that keeps the jaw in a position that reduces the likelihood of the throat closing. The sleep specialist indicated that the effectiveness of these appliances was only around 75 per cent, so he did not recommend them to his patients. As much as I respected his knowledge, I had to separate the science from the real life application of his recommended solution. By my calculations, 95 per cent effectiveness applied 0 per cent of the time equals 0 per cent effectiveness. By contrast, if I achieved 75 per cent effectiveness applied 100 per cent of the time by wearing the dental appliance nightly, I was achieving 75 per cent effectiveness. Pretty simple math. So I proceeded with a consultation on a dental appliance. Then I was faced with a tough financial decision: while the CPAP machine was fully paid for by the government health program, this dental appliance would cost me $2,300 and there was no reimbursement available from either the government or our employers' health plans. Once again, Rod's calm and rational approach encouraged me to invest in my health, quality of life, and longevity. We would find the $2,300. In the grand scheme of things, it really wasn't that much money to treat a condition that we knew was putting my life at risk.

To this day, I use my dental appliance about 98 per cent of the time, which by my calculations gives me a 70 per cent reduction in apnea episodes. This is perfectly acceptable to me. Dealing with my apnea reminded me that while health professionals are there to provide the information and the guidance, ultimately we must make our own educated decisions regarding our health.

In August of 2010, Rod and I both took on the Niagara Sprint Triathlon in Grimsby, Ontario; the same one I had completed in 2009. This year, I felt ready. Although there were always some minor nagging issues and tightness in various parts of my body, my continued discipline around nutrition and strength training was really paying off. I was also seeing Carm, the "magician" chiropractor at ISM, on a semi-regular basis to stay on top of any developing issues. I was doing yoga at least once a week. I used Epsom salt baths on days when I had a big workout or just felt a bit stiffer than usual, and used the ball and roller for 15–20 minutes daily to massage tight areas as needed. I generally felt good. There were no more incidents of pulling a muscle when doing things as benign as turning around too quickly or sweeping the front porch.

We had spent the day before the race carefully planning and filling our transition bags with wetsuits, shoes, socks, helmets, towels, snacks, race instructions, etc. We then drove to my brother's house for a sleepover since he and his wife had generously offered to babysit the girls and bring them to the race to cheer us on. We got up before dawn, looking forward to Rod's very first triathlon and to our first race together. What a treat to drive to the race with my husband and best friend beside me!

Once again, my goals were pretty modest. Although I had seen a lot of improvement, it was difficult to change more than thirteen years of programming that said: "Are you sure you should be doing this? What if you injure yourself again?" So my first goal was the same as last year: don't get injured! Secondly, I wanted to finish with a better time than last year. Thirdly, I wanted to be a little bit higher up in my age group rankings. It was interesting to compare my goals to Rod's, those of someone who did not have my history of chronic injury and pain. He was all about going as hard and fast as he could and achieving a respectable ranking within his age group. I winced at the thought of how hard he was going to push himself.

Although I was definitely nervous, it was so reassuring to have Rod there with me and to have the experience of having done it once before. We saw our friends Jean and Michael (both multiple IRONMAN race finishers) in the transition area during our race preparation. In addition to setting up my transition area, getting my body marked, and going to the porta-potty, I used the time to stretch and do some of Jillian's recommended activation exercises to get the muscles ready to perform. About thirty minutes before start time, we put on our wetsuits, and then headed toward the water. We spent a few minutes in the water warming up our strokes and trying to get the nerves out of our bodies. We kissed good luck and took up our places near the back of our respective age groups. Rod's group lined up a few groups behind mine.

Just before the gun went off to signal the start of my age group, we saw my brother Mike and his wife, Kerry, along with our daughters, on shore, waving and yelling out "good luck."

Although I had completed my Lake Ontario swim last year and knew what to expect, it wasn't much easier this time around. Having done all my training in a relatively empty swimming pool at a private club, this open water experience was overwhelming. I could feel my heart racing. I only completed about 50 to 100 meters of front crawl before switching to the breaststroke. The main difference this time was that my "go to" stroke was the breaststroke instead of the elementary backstroke. I probably did 75 per cent breaststroke and 25 per cent front crawl. There might have even been some elementary backstroke mixed in there, as I was pretty frazzled. Despite having clocked a lot of swimming time since my 2009 debut race, I only took about two minutes off my swim time (twenty minutes versus twenty-two). Once again, I was incredibly happy to be out of the water and moving on to the bike segment.

The most difficult part of the bike segment in Grimsby is climbing the Niagara Escarpment early on in the course. To this day, it is still the steepest climb I have ever encountered in all my miles of riding. As I labored up the monstrous first hill, Rod passed me looking incredibly intense and focused. He was giving it more than 100 per cent to ride up as fast as he could. I cheered him on as best I could, between gasps for air. I couldn't help but feel pride mixed with envy as I realized how well he must have done on his swim, not to mention the pace he was setting on the bike. Although I did expect him to be a bit faster on the bike, I had always been the faster swimmer during practice sessions. But Rod was always a game day performer. He could pull out performances that seemed beyond his ability when placed in a competitive situation. How I wished I could be more like him. As it turns out, his swim was almost one-and-a-half minutes faster than mine, despite the fact that he started swimming lessons eighteen months after I did, and our instructors agreed that my technique was stronger than his at this point. The difference was in his ability to push himself on race day. I realized I had a lot to learn about testing my limits. I needed to work on getting past my "I'm happy to finish without injury" mindset as my body got stronger and stronger. Despite my frustration with the swim, I took seven minutes off the previous year's overall race time and did achieve a better placement within my age group compared to the previous year. Goals accomplished. It was time to look ahead to what was next for us in the sport of triathlon.

One of the best parts of the race was seeing our beautiful kids' faces at the finish line. We were truly grateful to Mike and Kerry for having brought them. Rod loved the race experience and, like me after my first race, wanted to see how much better he could do if he trained harder and smarter. It was motivating to take on something totally new, because the prospects for improvement seemed unlimited. There was so much to learn about being a faster swimmer, cyclist, and runner. How far could we go? How much could we push ourselves?

Chapter 7—Looking Back: Lessons Learned

✓ Keep researching and learning more about your condition. I'm always surprised by how much new information I find every time I conduct a new search.

✓ If a solution offered by a health professional doesn't work for you after you've given it a solid try, don't give up on addressing the problem. Other solutions will present themselves to you as you continue the search.

✓ Make sure you push your health professional to present *all* the treatment options to you so that you can make the choice that will work best for your lifestyle. Physicians might steer you toward the treatment that has the best efficacy on paper, but what if it's a treatment that you can't tolerate, like the CPAP machine was for me?

✓ Don't delay on setting new goals for yourself as your health improves. However modest the goal, it is incredibly motivating to attain it, and this sets the stage for your next, higher level of achievement.

Chapter 7—Health Champion in Action

Chronic Obstructive Pulmonary Disease (COPD)—Or Not

Over the years, my mom's medical experiences have given me many opportunities to think about the need for self-advocacy in our health care system. One day, my mom discussed with her family doctor the occasional shortness of breath and wheezing she was sometimes experiencing in her late sixties and early seventies. In the doctor's opinion, my mom was suffering from COPD, a very serious lung condition that destroys lung function and capacity over time. COPD is normally found among long-time smokers or people exposed to asbestos. The last time my mom had had a cigarette was when she was twenty-nine years old. She had never lived in a house with asbestos insulation, nor had she ever set foot in an asbestos plant. I'm no doctor, but when she relayed her doctor's diagnosis to me, I was baffled. On what was he basing this diagnosis? My first question to my mom was: "Has your doctor ordered a lung function test?" Because the answer was no, I urged her to go back and request a lung function test and/or an appointment with a lung specialist.

I'm sure you can guess the outcome of the lung function test. What's fascinating is that her family doctor tried to insist that she stay on the powerful inhaler designed to treat COPD despite the normal lung function test results. Was he too lazy to think about what the real cause of her shortness of breath might be? This situation is a very good example of (1) the importance of asking questions when a diagnosis doesn't jive with your research, and (2) when it might be time to find another health professional who is interested in problem solving with you.

PUSHING THE LIMITS

After our positive 2010 race experience, it wasn't long before Rod and I were looking for our next triathlon challenge. The next day, we started planning our 2011 race season, setting our sights on an Olympic distance triathlon involving double the swim distance, and a 50 per cent longer bike and run segment compared to the sprint triathlon we had just completed.

In January 2011, we signed up to do five triathlons the upcoming summer. We decided to do two sprint races in preparation for our targeted Olympic race in mid-July. We aimed to round out the season with two additional sprint races later in the summer. We had the triathlon bug! That winter and spring, we worked closely with Jillian to make sure we were optimizing our strength workouts to be as strong as possible before racing season. We also discovered Coach Troy, a cycling coach who has excellent instructional videos we could follow while training on stationary bikes in our basement. We joined swimming clubs—each a different club so that one of us could be home with the kids—to improve our swimming stamina and speed. I was still running very little, as I was worried about incurring injuries that would hold me back for race season. As with my two previous races, my approach was to train hard with strength, bike, swim, and yoga, and basically run only when necessary (i.e., at the race).

Our first race of the 2011 season was in Woodstock, Ontario, on the weekend of June 10. We made a weekend out of it, since we wanted the kids to come with us. We arrived at our budget hotel on the Friday evening, and all had a great time jumping on beds and watching TV while eating our room service food. This is when we realized we could use triathlon weekends as a way to increase our family bonding time.

Rod was doing the longer sprint distance on the Saturday, and the kids were participating in a "Splash and Dash" swim / run event that afternoon. It was a cold and soggy day. The lakeshore was mucky and sprinkled with goose droppings, which the kids didn't particularly appreciate. Rod did really well in his race, finishing in the same time as his 2010 Niagara race, despite a 5 km longer bike course and almost 1 km longer run. He took three minutes off his 750 m swim compared to the previous year.

It was my turn to do the shorter sprint race on the Sunday. This involved a 500 m swim, 20 km bike, and 4 km run. I was really looking forward to what should have been a relatively easy race. As I entered the water, I could feel my heart rate climbing. Just like in the previous two races, within the first 100 m of the swim, I felt exhausted and overwhelmed. I felt even worse than last year. I began alternating between breaststroke and elementary backstroke. It took me eighteen minutes to complete 500 m, compared to twenty minutes for 750 m last year. Despite all the additional swimming in the pool over the winter and spring, I performed worse than ever in open water. I was very disappointed coming out of the water, though my performance on the bike and run were respectable. Right after the race, I told Rod there was no way I could do an Olympic triathlon in six weeks. If I could barely finish 500 m in open water, how could I possibly do 1,500 m? I might as well back out now rather than embarrass myself. We only had one more sprint race before the Olympic distance race in July. Rod calmly said to me: "All you need is open water practice. Let's find a place where we can practice open water swimming."

That very night, as soon as we returned home from Woodstock, Rod was on the computer looking up open water swimming in our area. He identified a few options, but it appeared as though a quarry in Caledon was the best choice. It was about a forty-minute drive from our house, and it was the training location for the Canadian Cross Training Club or C3 group that accepted all comers for a low membership fee. We signed up immediately and showed up at the first possible opportunity. We had to go separately, since most supervised swim times were early in the morning before work and someone had to be home with the kids. Showing up there with such little experience was pretty intimidating. Most people getting into the water appeared to be pretty accomplished triathletes. The buoys in the quarry were set up in a rectangle shape: 200 m from shore and 300 m apart. My goal for my very first time out was to swim the 200 m out to the first buoy, then turn around and come back for a total of 400 m. It seemed like it should have been a pretty easy task, since I could swim 1,500–2,000 m in the pool without stopping.

About halfway to the buoy, I felt that overwhelmed feeling again. I was gasping for air and turning to the breaststroke to catch my breath. As I approached the first buoy, I was panicking about my ability to turn around and swim back to the beach. Then I realized that the far shore was only about 10 m beyond the buoy in front of me. I got myself to that far shore and sat on a big rock to catch my breath and collect myself. *What am I doing here? I suck at swimming. This is so embarrassing.*

I then gathered the courage to swim back to my starting point, doing mainly the breaststroke. As much as I found the experience overwhelming and intimidating, I was very proud to have completed the 400 m. And deep down I knew that it could only get better with practice, as Rod had pointed out. I still had a couple of weeks until my next sprint triathlon, so I committed to coming back to the quarry at least twice more before the Welland Sprint Triathlon to be held on June 25 in my hometown of Welland, Ontario.

After two or three more visits to the quarry, I developed a swimming pattern that would give me a rhythm to focus on and that I could sustain for 750 m. I would do nine strokes of front crawl followed by two strokes of breaststroke, and I would keep repeating that pattern for the entire duration of the swim. This had two positive effects. The first was that having to count to nine and two allowed me to focus on the rhythm and reduce my anxiety. This was a trick I had used in tennis. I called it my mantra. I would repeat something in my head like "aggressive, confident, focused, relaxed" over and over again between points. This forced my brain to focus on the mantra instead of worrying about whether I was winning or losing. The second effect was that throwing in two strokes of breaststroke between every nine strokes of front crawl reassured me that I would get those extra breaths on a regular basis throughout the swim. Yes, it was a little unorthodox, but it seemed to work for me. I just wanted to complete an open water swim in which I swam front crawl for the majority of the distance without panicking and feeling overwhelmed. Before the Welland race, I made it once around the whole quarry (1,000 m) using my "nine and two technique." I was very excited about my improvement in open water swimming.

The Welland race turned out to be the perfect venue in which to build my confidence ahead of the seemingly overwhelming challenge of an Olympic triathlon. It is the only race I've ever been to in which swimmers enter the water one at a time. The swim is held in the Welland Canal. Because swimmers must go down a ladder to start, they enter the water one by one. This in itself was a stress reducer for me. I could establish my pace and rhythm right from the start, instead of worrying about getting out of the way of all the other arms and legs that are present during a mass start. In addition, the canal is a calm body of water with concrete embankments. It resembles a pool more than the lakes I had been in for the previous races. This was by far my best race to date in terms of personal satisfaction. Despite coming in last in my age group on the swim, my measure of success was how calm and relaxed I was coming out of the water. It was like night and day compared to the three previous races. My time was twenty minutes, about the same as my 2010 Niagara time for 750 m, but I felt so relaxed and energized coming out of the water, rather than frazzled and drained. This was a huge win for me.

I went on to complete the 30 km bike segment in one hour flat, which was by far my fastest bike segment ever, placing third in my age group for the bike. Considering I rarely did any run training, I was satisfied with my forty-two minutes for 7.5 km, which placed me eighth in my age group for the run. How far I had come in just three weeks! There was now a glimmer of hope in my mind that I could possibly complete the 1,500 m of open water in the upcoming Olympic triathlon by applying my nine and two technique, which kept me calm and feeling like I could go all day.

In the three weeks between the Welland and Gravenhurst triathlons I did several more quarry swims and continued to build my confidence with my patented swim technique. Rod developed a similar swim pattern ("ten and two") and we were both very excited when we each completed two laps of the quarry (2,000 m) the week before our July 16 race in Graven-hurst. Everything was lining up beautifully, and we had even convinced my best friend, MT; her husband, Andrew; and my brother Jehan to participate in the duathlon being held at the same venue. Their event consisted of a 2 km run instead of the swim, followed by the same 40 km bike and 10 km run that Rod and I would need to complete as part of our race. Once again, my brother Mike and his wife, Kerry, were our lifesav-ers. They agreed to spend the weekend at our house with the kids so that Rod and I could have a weekend away as part of our race adventure.

The race was being held on a Saturday, so MT, Andrew, Rod, and I all arrived at our hotel in Gravenhurst on Friday after-noon. We spent a few hours enjoying the sunshine and relaxing by the pool. Then we went for a drive to scope out the bike and run courses. The first thing we noticed was how hilly they were! The run was an "out and back" course. On the way out, everything seemed uphill, so we consoled ourselves with the thought that the way back would be mostly downhill. Jehan joined us for dinner that evening on a lovely patio overlooking Lake Muskoka. We all went to bed early to be ready for an early start the next morning.

We left our hotel at 6:15 a.m. to arrive in the transition area by 6:30. It would be our longest race yet. I expected to complete it in about three hours and fifteen minutes. I was still a little nervous about the swim and didn't know what to expect for the run, as I had only done a few training runs other than those in my sprint races. Not only was this my longest run in over fifteen years, but it was on a hilly course (I never did hill training) and the forecast called for a high of 28 degrees Celsius (about 82 Fahrenheit). Ultimately, the goal was just to finish: get through the swim, do well on the bike, and survive the run.

The most appealing part of this MultiSport Canada race was the swim start. Triathletes are taken out to the middle of Lake Muskoka on a steamship, where we all jump into the water and swim 1,500 m back to shore. What a fantastic experience getting on the old steamship hand in hand with Rod, alongside 298 other triathletes. My heart was pounding pretty hard, but I felt calmer than I had at the start of previous races because I knew I could rely on my nine and two swim technique to get me through the swim without panicking. The first wave of swimmers was called to jump off the ship and into the water around 7:55 a.m., with the start signal going off at 8:00 a.m. Every three minutes or so another wave was called. Rod was in a wave ahead of me. When my turn came, I jumped in and treaded water for a few minutes. There was a relatively small number of swimmers, so we could spread out and not crowd each other. The start gun went off, and I gradually found my nine and two rhythm. It was a beautiful sunny day on Lake Muskoka. For the most part it was glorious until we made a turn toward shore and the glare of the sun on the water made it nearly impossible to see where I was going. I started swimming off track, but luckily a lifeguard on a paddleboard indicated to me that I needed to adjust my course. A little more than forty minutes after the start, I was climbing up the ladder onto the dock and making my way toward the transition area to prepare for the bike segment. I felt great. It was the best swim of my life to this point. Yes, it was slow, but I had given myself a goal of forty-five minutes and I beat that goal. Good enough for me. No panicking, no extreme shortness of breath, and no need to turn on my back. I had just completed 1,500 m of swimming in open water! This was a glorious feeling.

Onto the bike. I had been training pretty hard on the bike since I was still hesitant to do any significant amounts of running. I thought I could complete the 40 km in about one hour and twenty minutes under ideal circumstances, but I knew that all the hills and the heat were going to make this goal pretty challenging. I rode like a madwoman. I was passing lots of people and felt great until the last fifteen minutes or so when I began to feel the heat and exhaustion. I wondered if I should reserve some energy for the 10 km run. It only took me a few seconds to come to the conclusion that the run would be brutal and slow no matter what, so I might as well give it everything I had to get a good bike time. I got off the bike in one hour and twenty-five minutes, which made me really happy given the tough conditions.

By the time I started the run it was approaching 10:30 a.m., and it felt really hot. I later learned the temperature had topped 30 degrees Celsius. The course felt even hillier than it had looked during our scouting drive the previous day. It was grueling. During the 5 km on the way out, I kept telling myself it would be much easier on the way back, as it would be mainly downhill. I walked many of the hills on that first half of the course. On the return, I kept looking for all the downhill relief I was supposed to be getting, but there didn't seem to be much of it. How could it be uphill in both directions? I was dying. My feet started to burn. I had to stop and ask the people at the water station for bandages for my blistering feet. I remember doing quite a bit of walking on and off. However, once I hit the 9 km mark I told myself to run the entire final kilometer. As I crossed the finish line, there were Rod, MT, Andrew, and Jehan waiting for me and cheering. What a feeling! A three-hour-and-twenty-four minute event. I had never done anything requiring such a long, sustained effort in my life. Just as I crossed the finish line and Rod came to greet me, I felt nauseated and dizzy. I said to Rod "I don't feel too good" and immediately sat down in the grass. I seemed to regain some strength, so I stood up again and walked over to where MT was sitting at a picnic table. As soon as I started to talk, I felt like I couldn't breathe. I sat down and she told me to put my head between my knees: her nursing training was kicking in. In that position, I felt okay. But the minute I would try to lift my head and/or do any talking, I felt as though I couldn't get any oxygen into my body. I was really feeling weak and dizzy.

MT walked me over to the paramedics tent where I was greeted by a somewhat arrogant EMT who sarcastically told his colleague: "She just swam, biked and ran for over three hours, so she's not feeling so good." I sat on their reclining chair, which made me feel much better. He took my blood pressure and said, "Your blood pressure is pretty low." Since my regular blood pressure was often in the range of 90/60 ("normal" usually being quoted as 120/80), I responded, "Oh yeah, it's usually on the low side."

"Is it usually around 57/43?" he asked.

"Oh no," I replied in a surprised voice, "it's not usually *that* low."

I was given some Gatorade and the attendant recommended that I go to the hospital.

The paramedics convinced me to get into the ambulance so that I could be taken to the hospital in Bracebridge, which was almost an hour away. As I waited for the ambulance driver to show up, a very nice female EMT did an ECG on me and monitored my blood pressure, which seemed to be rising as I remained lying down. With a normal ECG reading and my blood pressure on the rise, I really didn't want to waste my time going to the hospital. I had a feeling I would be fine if I just took it easy and drank lots of fluids for the rest of the day, so I asked to be released from the ambulance. I signed the waiver releasing the EMTs of all responsibility and called Rod to take me back to the hotel. Luckily he was still on site and came to pick me up. The last thing I wanted to do was ruin everyone's post-race celebration that afternoon by going to the hospital.

We all headed back to the hotel and did some lounging around the pool. I laid in the shade and drank lots of Gatorade while everyone else was enjoying beer, margaritas, and other adult libations. MT and Andrew's friends who owned a cottage just across Lake Muskoka from our hotel had offered to come and pick us up by boat and take us back to the cottage for some fun and frivolity. I felt too weak and exhausted to join, but insisted that the others go and have a good time. While the others drank too much beer and did crazy things like jumping off the cottage roof into the lake, I had a two-and-a-half hour nap and felt much better upon waking. I was able to join everyone for a nice dinner at the hotel restaurant and fell asleep easily that night.

Everyone assumed it was a hydration or electrolyte issue that had been responsible for my "episode" at the end of the race. However, in the back of my mind, I knew that I had been well hydrated. I urinated in the water during the swim (oops!), I drank lots of water and Gatorade during the bike segment, took some salt pills, and urinated again between the bike and run segments. I drank water every chance I got during the run as well. I seriously doubted it was a hydration issue. I might have bought into the possibility of it being an electrolyte imbalance. When I still wasn't feeling 100 per cent several days after the race, I decided to speak with my family doctor. According to her, I just overexerted myself, and I was fine now. My blood pressure was back to normal and there was nothing to worry about.

Rod and I had signed up to do the Niagara Sprint Triathlon in early August to be able to track our performance at the same race year over year. As the three weeks between the races passed, I really didn't feel up to doing the Niagara race. My energy level wasn't the greatest. Rod encouraged me to join him, so we got Rod's parents to come and babysit while we went to the race. The 750 m swim in Lake Ontario was grueling for me. I felt like

I couldn't breathe. On the bike, I felt completely exhausted. I had nothing to give. Halfway up the big hill near the beginning of the bike course, I had to stop, get off my bike, and struggle to get air into my lungs. I did get back on my bike and finished the race, but I experienced a completely new level of exhaustion. The encouraging thing is that, despite the exhaustion and stopping to catch my breath for several minutes on the bike, I was still faster than the previous year. When we got home I noticed blood on my socks and assumed I had a cut somewhere that I hadn't noticed. When I went to the bathroom, I realized my period had started during the race! I patted myself on the back for being such a warrior and attributed the exhaustion and shortness of breath to seasonal allergies, the start of my period, and the incomplete recovery from the Gravenhurst event.

The last race of our glorious 2011 triathlon season was in Lakeside, Ontario, near London on the weekend of September 17. I was doing the sprint event on Saturday, and Rod decided to tackle another Olympic distance race on the Sunday. Once again, we made it a family event and the kids signed up for their first real triathlon on the Saturday afternoon. We left our hotel early Saturday morning in what we believed was plenty of time to get to the transition area with about ninety minutes to spare. I wanted to have time to settle in, stretch, and warm up without feeling rushed. We followed the directions that had been provided on the race website, but it took us much longer than we expected to drive there, and I ended up placing my bike on the rack only thirty minutes before start time. I was a bit panicked. I had to use the porta-potty. Because I had spent much of the morning ensuring I was fully hydrated, my bladder was screaming. The porta-potty line up was at least ten minutes long. I still had to pick up my race kit and time chip, get my body markings, and put on my wetsuit. I did not have time to line up at the porta-potty. With ten minutes to go before the race start, it was time to put on my wetsuit. I had to pee so badly that I had to let it go while pulling on the wetsuit! I just hoped no one noticed the golden drops running out onto my lower legs.

As it turns out, the race organizers had to delay the start of the race because of the cold air and water temperatures. It was "wetsuit mandatory" meaning that those few athletes who planned to swim without one were not allowed to participate. I shivered as I waited for the organizers to decide whether the air temperature would climb enough to allow the race to take place. It was approximately 12 degrees Celsius (54 Fahrenheit) outside and the water was not warmer than 15 degrees C (59 F). About thirty minutes later, the start of the race was announced.

I checked my watch on my way out of the water; at seventeen minutes, my 750 m swim in the small, calm lake was my fastest yet. However, as I ran up to the transition area, I realized my hands were so frozen that I could not grip my wetsuit to pull it off! I had to rub my hands together and blow on them for several minutes before I could get them to function. When I finally got my suit off, it was a challenge to put on my cycling shoes. Once that was finally done, I tried to put on my gloves. My hands were so frozen and dysfunctional that I could not pull them on. I settled for a jacket to keep my body warm and started the bike ride with barely enough feeling in my hands to pull the brake handles if I needed to use them. Luckily, over the course of the 20 km bike ride, the sun warmed things up just enough for me to regain some feeling in my hands. I was satisfied with my bike time, and, except for a nagging feeling in one of my Achilles tendons, the 5 km run was uneventful.

To my surprise, I finished in eighth place out of sixteen women in my age group. This was my first time in the middle of the pack; I was used to being in the bottom quartile. This was the first time I started thinking about the possibility of being a contender in a race versus simply finishing. Maybe next season, I could think about bigger goals than just finishing without injury.

The kids and I cheered on Rod during his Olympic distance race on the Sunday. He did incredibly well, taking seventeen minutes off his time compared to the Gravenhurst event. He came out of the water in about thirty-three minutes, about five minutes sooner than I expected to see him, and he did particularly well on the run portion, coming in at forty-nine minutes for 10 km. This would have been a very good time for the run alone, never mind after a 1,500 m swim and a 40 km bike ride. So we both finished the season on a high note and looked forward to new breakthroughs in 2012.

Chapter 8—Looking Back: Lessons Learned

✓ A goal is something you cannot achieve today. I almost gave up on attempting the Olympic distance triathlon because I barely finished a 500 m swim six weeks before the race. Instead of saying "there's no way I can do that," you have to ask, "what do I need to do in order to achieve that?"

✓ Listen to that little voice in the back of your mind when you know something isn't right, and the answers you're getting from health professionals just don't seem to address the issue properly. I should have pushed harder to have some diagnostics done related to my Gravenhurst episode, especially when I had not fully recovered three weeks later.

Chapter 8—Health Champion in Action

Overwhelming Chest Pains in the Middle of the Night

In 2001, as I was preparing for fertility treatments, part of the protocol was to take an antibiotic (doxycycline) for several days prior to the start of the fertility treatments. One night, as I was drifting off to sleep, I remembered that I had not taken my doxycycline dose that day, so I got out of bed, took my pill, and went right back to bed. In the middle of the night, I woke up with horrible waves of pain across my chest. Having worked in the pharmaceutical industry for several years, I immediately suspected that the doxycycline pill could have gotten "stuck" in my esophagus when I laid down and caused some esophageal irritation. I went to the computer to look up "doxycycline and esophagitis" and sure enough there were reported cases of this and warnings about remaining upright for thirty minutes or more after taking the drug. I now had my diagnosis but had to do something about the unbearable pain, so I drove myself to the nearest hospital's emergency department.

As I described my symptoms to the triage nurse, she immediately sent me back to the examining area where I was hooked up to an ECG monitor. I assumed this was intended to rule out a heart attack. I had explained the doxycycline issue in detail, but she just blindly followed the chest pain protocol she had been trained to follow. At that point I thought: *I'm a thirty-five-year-old female who went to bed immediately after taking doxycycline, a drug known to cause esophageal irritation, and woke up with pain across the chest. Why wouldn't they first look down my esophagus instead of spending resources ruling out a heart attack? Is it just me or do you not need to be a medical specialist to figure this out? You just need to be a reasonable problem solver!*

Sure enough, the heart-related tests were negative and I finally convinced the attending physician that it was likely esophagitis caused by the doxycycline. He ordered an endoscopy and lo and behold, the esophagus was raw and irritated. He ordered painkillers and antacids to allow faster healing of the esophageal mucosa.

My take-away from this experience was that you are more likely to arrive at an effective solution if you give health professionals all the details surrounding the circumstances of your problem.

LIMITS? WHAT LIMITS?

Around October 2011, Rod and I discussed what our fitness and triathlon goals should be for 2012. Just as he had pushed us the previous year to set our sights on a more challenging event, Rod suggested that for 2012 we should train for a race that was half the distance of the well-known IRONMAN triathlons. As usual, I was the doubtful one. The swim didn't really scare me anymore, since the "half-iron" swim is 1,900 m, only 400 m more than the Olympic. I also knew I could get there on the bike (90 km). But I really didn't think I could do the run: a 21.1 km half-marathon. I had barely survived the 10 km run at the Olympic event! As before, Rod planted the seed, and my mind tried to wrap itself around the possibility. A few days later, Rod came home with a comprehensive triathlon-training guide for us to follow. It was just what I needed to buy into the whole idea. I thought to myself: *Okay, I'll just follow the training guide, and if it looks like I might be able to do it, I'll sign up for a half-iron race.* I shared this exciting dream with Jillian, my strength coach, and asked for her help in modifying my strength program to increase my chances of weathering a lot more running mileage. Up to this point, I had gotten away with showing up at races without any real run training. However, those days were over if I was seriously thinking of attempting a half-iron race.

In December, I told my friend MT about my crazy goal of doing a half-iron triathlon in 2012, and about the fact that I would need to start running more. In fact, I would need to sign up for a half-marathon in the spring of 2012 to test out my ability to go the distance on the run. She was thrilled. She jumped at the opportunity to do the half-marathon with me, so we signed up for the Toronto Goodlife Fitness half-marathon in May. Over the next few months, we would run side-by-side on treadmills at the gym every chance we got. We did a few outdoor runs together, but as the distances increased I could not keep up with MT's pace. (She is a long-time runner who has qualified for several Boston marathons.)

In January, once the half-marathon date was set, I decided to commit myself and actually register for a half-iron triathlon event. I wanted something as late in the summer as possible to give me a chance to (a) recover from the May half-marathon if I happened to get injured and (b) improve my swimming and biking as much as possible. My online search revealed a few races in Ontario in late August and early September. For some reason, I was drawn to a Somersault Event in Ottawa on Labor Day weekend. The date had not been confirmed at that point, so I went back a few weeks later to check on registration. The date had been confirmed for September 1—I almost fell out of my chair. September 1 was my dad's birthday, and he was born and buried in Ottawa. I broke into tears as I signed up for the race on the spot. This was meant to be. I would dedicate this race to my dad. When he died in 2005, I was not doing well at all. I was always in pain and discomfort, stretching and rolling on my tennis ball on the floor. This would be my way of showing him I was doing so much better than the last time he saw me.

On December 9, I left the company that acquired P&G Pharmaceuticals. Between December 2011 and May 2012, I took advantage of my newfound freedom from the corporate world. I ran more per week than I probably had in my life, and certainly since my early twenties, not to mention fitting in swim and bike workouts. However, I was conservative with my runs, rarely exceeding two per week, often only doing one per week. That being said, I was doing lots of strength and yoga training in between to protect myself from injury as much as possible. There were a few setbacks. Because of my tight hips and Achilles, my longest training run (and the longest run of my life to date) prior to the May half-marathon was 16 km. I had hoped to get close to 20 km before the event, but I had to settle with an injury-free 16 km. I had heard many times that it's better to be 10 per cent undertrained than 1 per cent overtrained. I continued to test this theory with just about every race I entered! I actually tended to be about 25 per cent undertrained, at least from the running perspective. Nevertheless, I really believed that I was better off making up for the lack of running with extra swimming and cycling, which worked my cardiovascular fitness without the excess strain on my joints and soft tissues.

On May 6, 2012, at the age of forty-six, I participated in my first half-marathon. As MT and I drove to the event, I reflected on the fact that somewhere between 1996 and 2008 I had given up on the thought of ever doing an endurance event such as a marathon or triathlon. In the deep recesses of my conscious mind, however, there was a very meek voice that would once in a while pipe up with something like: *maybe a half-marathon some day,* but that would usually get squashed by the bigger voice that said: *forget it, this body will never cooperate.* In 2008, MT had mentioned that if I ever felt well enough to do a half-marathon, she would do it with me. At the time, I thought: *that's really nice of her, but not likely going to happen.* And now here we were, shivering in the early morning hours, along with thousands of other runners. I was about to attempt a 21.1 km run for the first time in my life. My goals for this one were: (1) Don't get injured, (2) finish, and (3) ideally, run the whole thing without stopping or walking.

Within the first kilometer or so, there was a significant uphill section. My legs felt heavy and tired. *Oh no, this might not be my day. Let's just try to get to the top of this hill and see how things go.* My heart was pounding as I tried to catch my breath at the top of the hill. I knew that most of the course was on a gentle downhill slope, so I kept running at what felt like a snail's pace, looking for relief as the course flattened out. By this point, I had waved MT on. I wanted her to find her pace and do her best. A few kilometers past that first hill, I started to find a comfortable pace and played the most inspiring songs on my iPod. It seemed to get easier with each kilometer. Before I knew it, I was at the 16 km mark: my longest distance completed until that day. I quickly turned my thoughts to the fact that there were only 5 km remaining. I had done 5 km many times before. This was going to be easy! With 1 or 2 km to go, I saw some people walking. *You've come all this way, what a shame to start walking now.* I ran all the way to the finish and completed my first half-marathon in a very respectable two hours and twelve minutes. I felt overjoyed, and this was now my proudest moment to date, as running had been my nemesis. MT was there to greet me—she completed her run in 1:50—and we celebrated together. I now had the belief that I could complete a half-iron triathlon! Now that the run was conquered, I was pretty sure the swim and bike were possible. Time to get training for Ottawa.

Some time during the summer of 2012, I was on the trampoline in our backyard with my youngest daughter, Sabrina. She was doing cartwheels on the trampoline. I remember saying to her:

"I've never been able to do a cartwheel."
Her response was, "I can teach you."

"No, thanks," I said. "I don't want to do anything too crazy before my big race."

She then said, "If you ever do a full IRONMAN, then you will have no excuse and you will need to learn how to do a cartwheel."

I said: "Okay, that's a deal. I don't think I'll ever be able to do an IRONMAN, so I'm pretty safe."

By this time, I had been working with Jillian for almost three years. I had made immense progress in my strength-training program by going from strictly trying to improve range of motion, stability, and balance to actually building some real strength with Olympic weightlifting moves. My thigh muscles felt thick, and I had muscles in my glutes and upper back that I never knew existed. To think that in my twenties I exercised to be thin! Now, I looked at the strong muscles all over my body and thought: *Bring it on! The thicker and stronger, the better. It means I'm strong and I won't break anymore.* I was fitter than I had ever been in my life and felt younger than ever at age forty-six.

I had a very disciplined training schedule, thanks to the manual Rod had bought us. With two young children, searching for a new career, and a less than perfect body, I made several modifications to the recommended training program. I did about 75 per cent of the swimming and cycling workouts and maybe 30 per cent of the running recommended in the guide. However, I was adding three strength workouts and one yoga class per week. On top of that there were my chiropractor visits every three to four weeks, rolling with the ball and the roller every night, and getting the odd massage. It was a busy summer leading up to the Ottawa half-iron race. Right up until the event, it felt like I was dreaming whenever I would tell people that I was training for a half-iron triathlon. My brain wasn't really buying it.

The summer 2012 triathlon plan was to do one race in June, the Gravenhurst Olympic distance again in July, then I would do my half-iron race in Ottawa on Labor Day weekend and Rod would do his big one in Muskoka, Ontario, on September 9. We chose the Guelph Lakes triathlon in mid-June as our first race of the season. Rod opted for an Olympic distance while I chose to do a sprint. It was another family triathlon weekend, which we all really enjoyed. My race was first on the Saturday and I kicked butt. I was starting the season better than I could have dreamed. My overall placement was eleventh out of thirty-eight women in my age group. I was twenty-third in the swim (compared to consistently among the last three out of the water), fifth on the bike, and fifteenth on the run. For the first time in my triathlon history, I came in with a time that was faster than the average time for all participants, both men and women. I actually allowed my mind to wander into the realm of a possible podium finish in the near future.

Rod took another five minutes off his best Olympic race time from the previous year. His gains came from faster swim and bike times, while his run time remained about the same. But something happened during that race. Although his left hip had been giving him trouble for years, he had been managing it with strength training, chiropractics, and anti-inflammatories. After the Guelph race, the pain became more intense and running became very painful for him. During the month of July, his hip was so sore and inflamed that even walking was difficult at times.

Also after the Guelph race, I began developing some unusual symptoms on the left side of my chest. The Monday morning after race weekend, I felt as though something was squeezing my chest on the left side. I felt some pain and discomfort down my left arm and up into my neck. I immediately thought that I might be having a heart attack. The symptoms seemed to fit, and they were coming after a high exertion event. Rod took the kids to school, and I drove myself to the hospital. I was taken

My McMaster University varsity tennis team circa 1987. That's me, top second from left.

My beloved Dad was ecstatic when he got to hold his first grandchild.

New Years 1999. Sitting was so uncomfortable, I would pull my shoulders up and forward in an attempt to stretch the sides of my body.

I loved to hike on vacation, even when it hurt. This is me in Greece, taking one of my frequent stretch breaks.

One of my classic "lying down" poses, though I preferred the floor!

The girls knew to find me on the floor. That's where we often played.
Below: I still like going horizontal, but thankfully not because of pain.

PHOTO by Get to the Point Media

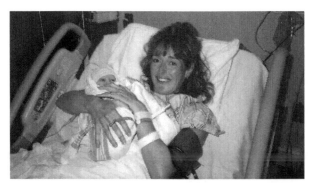

My first miracle baby arrives in 2002.

Pride, joy and love on Rod's face, holding Arquelle at 2 weeks.

Below: Arquelle is not sure about having to share the floor with little sister!

Back to Dr. Schoolcraft's office in 2012 for the first time since 2003, when Sabrina was conceived. What a great feeling to introduce our girls to him and thank him for his help in making our miracles come true.

Rod and I completed our first 4-hour bike ride, spring of 2013. How great it's been to have him by my side through all the ups and downs of pushing my physical limits.

Left: MT and me at the half marathon in 2012. Could not have done it without her support.

My sweet girls (and Rod—behind the camera) cheered me on all day at the 2012 half-iron race in Ottawa.

August 18, 2013 in Mont Tremblant, Quebec. A key turning point in my life. I had to dig deep on the bike and the run, but somehow I knew I was going to make it.

3 PHOTOS by FinisherPix.com

Left: I spot Rod and the kids in the crowd just before crossing the finish line at Subaru IRONMAN North American Championship Mont Tremblant. Right: Crossing the finish line, all the pain and exhaustion melt away as I think to myself: "I want to do another one!"

I swam 2.4 miles, biked 112 miles and ran 26.2 miles in fourteen hours and forty-seven minutes. Well under the seventeen hour limit. When I held that finisher medal I thought back on what it took to get here and it was then I knew my new life was just beginning.

3 PHOTOS by FinisherPix.com

immediately for an ECG and blood work. After a long wait, I was given an echocardiogram (heart imaging using ultrasound) and was told by the attending physician that I had some pericarditis, which is inflammation in the pericardium, the tissue that surrounds the heart. This really scared me. There's a problem with my heart? I didn't get much information at all from this physician, who offered me Aspirin to treat the inflammation and the name of a cardiologist with whom I needed to book an appointment. I told him that I had previously suffered a gastrointestinal bleed with ibuprofen and that I really didn't want to take any chances with Aspirin. He gave me a few days' worth of prednisone instead.

When I got home, my head was spinning. I started to do all the research I could about pericarditis and the outcomes associated with it. They ranged anywhere from going on to live a normal life to serious heart damage. Everything I read confirmed that Aspirin or prednisone were the therapies of choice. I was feeling somewhat better by the next day, and I assumed it was the prednisone kicking in.

I had recently seen Dr. Galea to review what had happened to me in Gravenhurst in 2011. I wanted to make sure there weren't any serious underlying issues as I prepared for a six hour or longer half-iron race in September. After I had recounted the Gravenhurst event to Dr. Galea, he immediately looked at my blood tests that had been done some time in 2010. He noticed that my ferritin (blood iron) level was quite low at that time and felt that this could have been responsible for what he called my "syncope" episode in 2011. Without enough iron stores, your body can't make sufficient hemoglobin, which is the oxygen carrier in your blood. In 2010, my ferritin level measured 22 mcg/ml. What the lab report failed to point out is that ferritin levels between 12 and 30 represent depleted iron stores.

However, this report showed a ferritin "reference range" of 10 to 300. For a couch potato, a ferritin level of 22 would likely never present itself as a problem. I'm starting to believe that most tests and treatments in our medical system are geared toward couch potato aspirations. A "reference range" does NOT mean a "normal" range; it only indicates the range of findings within the population. The reference range has absolutely nothing to do with whether your results are acceptable for your current or planned lifestyle and level of activity. They certainly don't represent acceptable ranges for an endurance athlete.

When Dr. Galea re-did my ferritin test, it showed that the level had dropped to 16 mcg/ml, very close to the point of serious deficiency. He told me that as an endurance athlete, I needed to have my ferritin up near 100. This knowledge was doing a lot to explain what happened in Gravenhurst. The immediate action was to start taking high doses of iron supplements and measure my ferritin level again in three or four months.

Given the recent pericarditis diagnosis, I wondered if the Gravenhurst episode could have been related to my heart problem in addition to the iron deficiency. As a precaution, Dr. Galea arranged for me to see a cardiologist, so I did not book the appointment with the cardiologist recommended by the ER physician. When I walked into the cardiologist's office, I was greeted by a rude technician. She conducted an echocardiogram and then told me I was going to have a stress test done, which would involve running on a treadmill while they observed what was happening with my heart rhythm and conduction patterns. Having just been to the ER believing I had pericarditis and still having some pain on the left side of my chest, I asked if I could speak to the doctor before doing the stress test. The technician gave me an annoyed look, rolled her eyes, and told me to have a seat in the waiting room. Then the best part came. When I spoke with the cardiologist, he abruptly told me my heart looked fine and there was no evidence of fluid in the pericardium. He told me that pericarditis "happens" and that I just needed to finish taking the steroids prescribed by the ER physician. He gave me no information on what to expect next. When he realized that he couldn't whisk me out of his office right away, he gave me a few minutes to describe my historical episodes. He assured me that those were likely unrelated to this (suspected) pericarditis event, and that I was probably just "pushing my body past its limits". He told me that I needed to stop pushing myself so hard when I worked out and stop reading so much stuff on the internet. His advice was to just finish up the prednisone, not worry about any recurrence issues with pericarditis, and to only work out to the point where I didn't get those symptoms. What the hell did that mean? Could I safely train for a six-hour triathlon event or not? I was shocked and angry walking out of that appointment. That night, I wrote a letter to Dr. Galea suggesting that he should reconsider sending his patients to that cardiologist.

After the prednisone tablets were gone, the discomfort and pressure on the left side of my chest returned. I told my family doctor that I was feeling a bit weak and had this "squeezing" feeling in my chest. Since the current thought was that I had pericarditis, she suggested Aspirin. I explained my history of GI bleeding, but she insisted that enteric-coated Aspirin would be fine. Having worked as a pharmaceutical representative on a product that protected the stomach from anti-inflammatory-induced bleeding, I knew that enteric coating was not sufficient to prevent a GI bleed. The anti-inflammatory drug's effect on the stomach lining is systemic and is not related to any irritation caused by direct contact with the tablet. The same holds true for Aspirin. But I didn't have the energy to argue with my doctor, so I followed her suggestion and started taking Aspirin a few times per day for the next several days.

Around the fifth day, I woke up in the middle of the night feeling nauseated and sweaty. I made it to the toilet just in time to vomit chunks of bright red blood. Immediately, my mind went to thinking this was somehow related to my heart problem. I felt so weak and sick. I had to call out to Rod who was sleeping in the adjoining room and ask him to take me to the hospital for my second visit to the ER in less than two weeks. This time I was treated very differently. After the immediate ECG and blood work (standard when a possible heart attack is suspected), I was sent to a hospital bed and hooked up to a monitor. The attending physician seemed like a really good problem solver. He took a thorough history and explained to me all of the things they needed to rule out, including a heart problem and the possibility of a pulmonary embolism (blood clot in the lung). Several tests were done, including a more sophisticated echocardiogram and a CT scan. They kept me hooked up to monitors until a cardiologist was available. They were preparing an in-patient bed to keep me overnight when the cardiologist showed up. This guy was a breath of fresh air. He reviewed all of my test results and asked me a lot of good questions about my health history, including questions about my fitness training. He then proceeded to give me his opinion based on a pretty complete picture of my situation.

Dr. Tiong's opinion was that I was having muscle spasms across the left side of my chest. He had seen this before in cyclists, who spend time in a forward and somewhat hunched position. Given my history of myofascial pain and stiffness and my increasing mileage on the bike, this would make sense. All of my test results were negative for any heart or lung condition that might have been consistent with my symptoms. He also explained that everyone has a bit of fluid in the pericardium, and his review of my echocardiogram didn't cause him any concern related to pericarditis. As for vomiting blood, given my history of GI bleeding, he concluded that this was a GI bleed caused by the Aspirin.

His conclusions and explanations made so much sense. I wished our entire health care system could be populated with professionals like him: true problem solvers. Really good doctors are so rare, but you know them when you meet them. When their explanations are thorough and clear and everything seems to fall into place as they go through the explanation, you know you've found a good doctor. Dr. Tiong recommended doing a lot of chest opening stretches. This is something I had not spent much time on, so I vowed to be more thorough with my stretching and rolling. After seeing such a competent problem solver, I felt totally confident that I did not have a heart problem and I could go back to training as hard as I wanted to fulfill my half-iron triathlon dream. Imagine if I hadn't had the second episode and had not met Dr. Tiong. I might have drifted along for several months, trying to get an appointment with another cardiologist, thinking I needed to completely back off triathlon training or at least "not push myself" as the previous cardiologist had suggested. And while another cardiologist might have also ruled out pericarditis and given me a free and clear report on heart issues, it is unlikely he or she would have taken as comprehensive a problem-solving approach as Dr. Tiong. My "chest squeezing" symptoms could have persisted and even progressed, leaving me struggling and unsure of how much training I should be doing. This is the life-changing impact of a superior health professional. Thank you, Dr. Tiong.

By this point, it was the first week of July. Both Rod and I were registered for the Gravenhurst Olympic distance triathlon on July 14. We had planned for my friend Corrine to come and spend the weekend with our daughters, much to their delight. Until this point, I had seriously doubted my ability to do the race, and Rod's hip was so painful that he was ready to pull out as well. After Dr. Tiong's review of my test results and perceptive conclusion that I had a soft tissue problem and not a heart problem, I was totally ready to take on Gravenhurst. Given my reduced training volume over the three weeks while all this health drama was happening, I didn't have any performance expectations. But I thought it would be a great training race in preparation for my Ottawa race. Plus, it was a great opportunity for a date weekend with Rod. I talked Rod into completing the swim and bike part of the race and then just pulling out of the run. The goal of participating in the race was just to enhance our training at this point. He still had hopes of being able to participate in the half-iron distance race in Muskoka in September.

We had a really nice weekend in Gravenhurst. Being familiar with the race and having no expectations meant that we were surprisingly relaxed on race morning. I shocked myself by taking eighteen minutes off my 2011 race time. I felt awesome. This really reinforced the importance of not overtraining and tapering for the few weeks ahead of any race. The other factor leading to my success was being relaxed and having no expectations. This was a lesson to take with me in all aspects of life. Rod had a fantastic swim and a solid bike before calling it a day and cheering me on at the finish line. My ever-supportive brother and sister-in-law who have a cottage close to Gravenhurst even joined Rod at the finish line. These guys gave up their day to be there for us again. Incredible.

With no improvement in his hip symptoms, Rod booked a consultation with Dr. Galea, who ordered a high resolution MRI. Two weeks before the Muskoka race, Dr. Galea informed Rod that he had moderately severe osteoarthritis in both hips, although the left one was worse than the right. His options were as follows:

OPTION 1 — Stop running, take no surgical action, keep taking anti-inflammatories as needed, and he would be able to put off total hip replacement surgery for many years;

OPTION 2 — Consider hip resurfacing surgery, after which the medical community doesn't recommend running, but many athletes who undergo the procedure continue with their high-impact sports; or

OPTION 3 — Total hip replacement, after which there would definitely be no running allowed.

Rod's choices were clearly #1 or #2. At age forty-eight, there was no way he would consider a total hip replacement. Hip replacements last a maximum of twenty years, and the success rate on the second replacement is much lower than the first. Doing a total hip replacement today meant possible debilitation around age sixty-five. We plan to still be very active at age sixty-five, so no thanks! Hoping to find some answers, Rod accepted Dr. Galea's offer to book a consultation with a top hip-resurfacing expert in Canada. Just a few weeks earlier we had met a fellow triathlete who had both hips resurfaced and was back to running and triathlons in his mid-fifties. Everything sounded great until Dr. Schemitsch pointed out that the resurfacing procedure has the best chance of success on patients with femurs (thigh bones) with a diameter of more than 5 cm. In order to be placed on the waiting list for hip resurfacing, Rod would have to sign an agreement saying that if, once the procedure was started, Dr. Schemitsch found that the femur was not large enough, he could do a total hip replacement. This was not a straightforward decision. When we asked about determining femur diameter without cutting, Dr. Schemitsch explained that x-rays give approximate measures but the error rate can be quite high. Although Rod's x-ray showed a femur diameter over 5 cm, there were no guarantees of what would be found once surgery began.

As all of this information was sinking in, Rod decided to pull out of the Muskoka event. This was difficult for both of us, as we were really enjoying setting goals and training together. He was such a good runner and enjoyed it so much (when not in pain). It broke my heart to see him robbed of this great sport. However, being the positive, can-do guy that he is, the mourning only lasted a few weeks. His mind turned to thoughts like: "Maybe I can't run. But what *can* I do?" He looked up all of the triathlon events that had swim-bike events built in. To our surprise, almost all of the triathlons included a swim-bike event for the 2013 season. This option is attractive because the athlete gets an official swim-bike finishing time, versus simply pulling out of a triathlon prior to the run portion and getting a DNF (did not finish) beside their name on the posted results. So Rod looked forward to continuing his swimming and cycling training with the goal of entering swim-bike events coinciding with my triathlon events the following year.

Rod put his name on the waiting list for hip resurfacing, however, his current thinking is that he will manage his hip pain with strength and flexibility training as well as anti-inflammatories when needed. As long as the pain is managed and he is not driven to run again, then it makes sense to delay a surgery with uncertain outcomes. The important thing is that he took action, made sure he understood the diagnosis and the options, and made a conscious choice. It is in his best interest to stay away from high impact sports like running and tennis, but there is no reason why he can't still be strong and fit with strength training, yoga, swimming, cycling, and anything else he chooses in the future. The stronger his hip muscles, the more his hip joint is supported and the less pain he will feel. In turn, this means keeping up with his young daughters, whether it is at the amusement park, playing in the backyard, or walking on the beach on a tropical vacation. That is the incentive for pushing on, staying fit, and not letting his "bad hip" drag him down. That is his "why."

With the fear of a possible heart problem behind me and a fresh reminder that chronic myofascial pain syndrome is something that can be managed but not cured, I picked up my half-iron training program where I had left off before Gravenhurst. My confidence was building every day. I was starting to believe I could potentially complete the 1,900 m swim doing mostly front crawl. I felt strong on the bike, and although my running mileage was well below that recommended in the training program, the memory of my recent half-marathon finish gave me the confidence to believe the run would not be a barrier for me. I started paying more attention to using the roller and ball to massage all major muscle groups, in both the upper and lower body. I asked Jillian for advice on shifting my strength program toward some more back strengthening and chest opening moves. Just the thought of completing a half-iron triathlon on my dad's birthday in the city where he was born and buried brought tears to my eyes. The thought crossed my mind often. Lots of tears were shed in the months leading up to September 1. One of the items I added to my packing list was a black Sharpie marker. I would write *Daddy* on my arm before the race so that I could draw strength from him throughout the event.

August 30 was packing day. My period had started the previous day, which meant that there was something else to think about on race day. My good friend Donna was visiting and we were hanging out by the pool in our backyard while my kids were swimming with her son. As was always the case with Donna and my good friends, I felt a sense of support, encouragement, and nothing but positive vibes as I prepared for the biggest physical challenge of my life. She stayed with me as I packed, even making a trip to the store for various feminine products to help me pack for the over six hour race. She had lots of good suggestions, and we came up with the best possible "protection and quick changeover" strategy for me.

On August 31, we loaded up the car for a weekend trip to Ottawa. The excitement was palpable. My support crew of three were primed for the adventure. I had to keep pushing back that annoying voice in my head that kept saying: "Are you sure you can do this? You can always back out and everyone would understand." For most of the six-hour car trip, I was running FSM protocols on my portable machine, ensuring my body was in the best possible condition for the race. I was paying very strict attention to hydration, alternating between water and an electrolyte drink all the way. The cooler was packed with all the protein-rich healthy snacks I could think of.

We drove straight to the cemetery in Ottawa to say hi to my dad. Rod and I had a good cry as the girls arranged and rearranged the flowers on the grave and tried to cheer me up. All I could think of saying to my dad was "I'm okay, Dad, see? I'm doing a half-iron triathlon tomorrow!" From the cemetery, we drove to the Terry Fox Athletic Facility for the orientation session at 5 p.m. I picked up my race kit and listened to the organizers take us through the rules and instructions, noting as many details as possible in order to not be stressed and confused at start time.

Dinner that night was at a restaurant near the hotel. I chose chicken, rice, and cooked vegetables: pretty much my standard pre-race dinner, except that I sometimes chose salmon instead of chicken. Back at the hotel, Rod and the kids watched a movie while I prepared my drink bottles and snacks and reviewed my checklist to ensure everything I needed was in my transition bag. I joined my family for the last thirty minutes of the movie as I rolled out my muscles with the roller and the ball. Throughout the evening, I continued to pay close attention to hydration.

Given the 6:30 a.m. start time, I needed to arrive in transition around 5:00 a.m. to start my race day routine. I always gave myself ninety minutes to set up shoes, helmet, sunglasses, drinks, snacks, salt pills, Tylenol, and the seemingly endless number of items I would need to get through the three legs of the race. For this particular race, I had to pay attention to the complicating factor of having a tampon handy for the transitions. For the first time, I had written out a detailed list of what I needed at which point in the race, so as not to miss anything. After all, this race was about twice as long as my previous longest.

After picking up the race cap and doing body markings, I returned to my spot in the transition area to write *Daddy* on my left forearm with the Sharpie marker I had packed. He would be there with me the whole way. I then proceeded to stretch, drink, and eat one last snack before using the porta-potty and putting on my wetsuit. I walked down to Mooney's Bay on the Rideau River to prepare for start time. As I made my way down to the beach, I spotted Rod and the kids; their happy faces warmed my heart. The butterflies in my stomach were beginning to go wild. As I approached Rod, he leaned into my ear and whispered: "Just remember, you've already won." As soon as he said that, my entire body relaxed. My heart rate must have dropped by forty beats per minute. I could breathe so much easier. He was so right. *I'm here! I'm at the start line of a half-Iron triathlon.* Just a few years ago, all I wanted was to run a couple of kilometers without injury or spend a day without struggling to find a comfortable position. This was beyond my wildest dreams. What could I possibly be nervous about?

It was a beautiful, sunny day, a bit cool this early in the morning but I looked forward to a forecasted 22 degrees Celsius (72 Fahrenheit). I was shin-deep in the water as the countdown started. The start gun went off and 122 of us walked, ran, and dove in for our 1,900 m swim. Within a few minutes, my dad's face appeared in front of me. The swim felt so easy, so effortless as if he were pulling me along. Since the course was a rectangular shape, we swam both with and against the current at various times. But I felt like I was going with the current for the entire swim. Up until that day, not only had my longest race swim been 1,500 m, but I had never completed an open water swim doing 100 per cent front crawl. I found myself in the last 400 m still doing front crawl and passing people doing the breaststroke. *That's usually me!* I had hoped to do the swim in fifty minutes and came out of the water in forty-eight minutes feeling totally refreshed.

I alternated between jogging and walking the kilometer or so to the transition area, high-fiving my cheering section along the way. In transition, I pulled off my wetsuit, put on my socks, cycling shoes, sunglasses, and helmet, took a salt pill along with some sips of water and a few bites of a protein bar, and ran out with my bike to the sweet sound of my family's cheers.

The bike course consisted of six loops of 15 km each, ideal for spectators and for the athletes who could draw strength from their cheering section several times throughout the 90 km ride. Having heard that the course was quite flat, I had set a goal to average 30 km per hour and complete the ride in three hours. This was aggressive, given the lost training time spent grappling with a suspected heart problem. I made sure I was fully hydrated and nourished throughout the ride and never let my heart rate drop below 160 bpm, an effort level I was pretty sure I could sustain for three hours. I never had to make a potty stop, had my cheering section there every 30 minutes, and had the ride of my life finishing in three hours and three minutes.

Back into transition, I took off my bike helmet, changed into my running shoes, drank and ate some more, and made a necessary porta-potty visit to prepare for the more than two hours of running ahead of me. I felt pretty drained at this point and tried not to think too much about the fact that I was about to start running a half-marathon. There were four loops, each a little more than 5 km. Each loop finished in front of the grandstands where spectators would cheer for us. Rod and the kids were still there for me, totally focused on cheering me on every time they saw me.

My first loop and a half were amazing, and I was on track for a two hour half-marathon. My goal was 2:20. But during the back half of the second loop, I felt burning under my feet that started to slow me down. As I entered the stadium at the end of the second loop, I couldn't see Rod and the kids in their usual spot. My heart sank, as I really needed the morale boost at that point. Just as I made the turn to head back out of the stadium, I heard my name called, looked back and there they were waving to me.

My pace picked up for a while as I basked in the joy of having such an incredible family behind me. But halfway through that third loop, the pain became so intense I started to feel some nausea. I asked a volunteer at the water station if anyone had any bandages. One person did and offered them to me. I was so grateful. I stopped, took my shoes and socks off, and put a couple of bandages under each foot. This helped me finish the third loop with less pain. It still hurt like hell and I called on my dad for help many times. Soon my thoughts turned to the fact that I was lucky to be alive and that the pain only served to remind me that I was alive. So I welcomed the pain as a confirmation of my presence among the living and an offering to my dad. Starting the fourth lap, the pain became excruciating again. I hobbled along, walking a few segments until I reached the water station with the helpful volunteer. A few negative thoughts started to cross my mind. Imagine if I couldn't finish, with less than 3 km to go on the entire race! I couldn't let my mind go there. I would walk if I had to and still make it within the cut-off time. It would be disappointing given how well I had done so far, but no matter what, I would finish and I would be grateful.

The lady who had helped me with the bandages offered a lubricating cream that might help alleviate the unbearable burning sensation on the bottoms of my feet. Once again, the shoes and socks came off; I took off the bandages and rubbed the cream into the soles of my feet. As I started to run again, there was significantly less pain and I could run the remaining 2.7 or so kilometers to the finish.

My half-marathon time was 2:34 for a total race time of 6:34. I was extremely happy with this result, given the circumstances. Approaching the finish line, I heard the announcer call out my name and say: "Come on, get those arms up" and I obliged, just as the official photographer snapped my finishing photo. With both arms in the air, the look on my face said it all. It was pride, relief, exhilaration, and disbelief. The emotions overcame me as I thanked my dad for being there with me. I crumbled into a chair at the paramedic's tent to catch my breath. The paramedic rushed toward me, asking if I was Okay. I nodded yes with a huge grin on my face. I grabbed a banana and a water bottle, and then returned to the bleachers to hug Rod and the kids. Despite the exhaustion, I felt amazing. I even had the energy to go out for a celebration dinner with Rod and the kids that night. Before nodding off to sleep, I sent out the following email to my close friends and family:

To my positive and supportive friends,

Today was one of the most incredible days of my life. Not only did I complete my first half-iron race (1.9 km swim, 90 km bike, and 21.1 km run), but I did it in Ottawa, where my Dad is buried, on my Dad's birthday. It was a beautiful sunny day. Rod and the kids were on site for over 8 hours, and cheered me on with high energy for 6.5 hours while I completed my race. They are amazing, and I am blessed to have them.

However, I am also blessed to have incredible people like you in my life. In one way or another, each one of you has contributed to my ability to accomplish something like this. Do not underestimate your positive influence on people's lives!

The swim was my best ever in terms of feeling relaxed and completing it with relative ease, 2 minutes faster than my goal time. I felt strong on the bike, and met my time goal. The run was really tough because of developing blisters on the underside of my feet. Despite having to stop a few times for Band-Aids and Vaseline, I was able to complete the 21.1 km in about 2.5 hours (goal was 2 hrs 20 mins). My total time was 6 hours and 34 minutes.

I love you all, and thank you for all your positive energy and support. More than anything, thanks for being part of my life.

Love,
Carole

Chapter 9—Looking Back: Lessons Learned

✓ Don't accept vague statements from health professionals, such as "don't push yourself" without a clear explanation behind it. Ask them to give you specific advice with the rationale behind it. If the explanation doesn't sound right to you, do some additional research and seek another opinion.

✓ Make it clear to your health professional that you want to understand all the options available to you, so that you can make an informed decision that best suits your lifestyle and your long term life goals.

✓ If a doctor tells you to stop reading so much stuff on the internet or doesn't answer your questions to your satisfaction, keep looking. You haven't found the right doctor yet.

✓ If you're motivated to work toward an athletic feat that is out of your reach today, look for a credible training program designed by a professional in the sport you're pursuing. Be sure to adapt that training program according to your body's strengths and weaknesses. Remember: it's better to be 10 per cent undertrained than 1 per cent overtrained.

✓ Always review your medical test results. If anything seems to be at the top or bottom of a "reference range," bring it to your doctor's attention and ask questions about it. Ask about whether it could make a difference to your fitness goals. Make it clear to your doctor that you want to do more than just survive: you want to thrive.

Chapter 9—Health Champion in Action

Infertility

A few years ago, a good friend of mine expressed his frustration with the fertility problems he and his wife were having. They had been trying for several years and recently started going to a local fertility clinic. Theirs was a very complex infertility case. After many failed treatments, he asked me for information about the Colorado Center for Reproductive Medicine, where my two girls were successfully conceived after several failed attempts elsewhere. I was thrilled that he asked and enthusiastically provided him with the contact information. There was no question in my mind that Colorado would give them the best odds of success based on the research I had done for myself in the past.

After making a number of trips to Denver and following the protocol prescribed by Dr. Schoolcraft, I am very excited to report that my friend and his wife are now proud parents of beautiful twins. One of the key factors my friend noted about his experience with Dr. Schoolcraft was that he always got a thorough explanation about why and how the recommended treatments addressed their specific fertility problem.

In my experience, worthy health professionals are problem solvers who always provide recommendations and explanations that make sense. They welcome your questions and are either able to answer them knowledgeably or to direct you to someone better equipped to answer them.

10

THE ADVERSITY ADVANTAGE

At the end of 2012, I had been "retired" from my corporate job for almost a year and was still searching for exactly what I wanted to do with my life. Having obtained my realtor's license, I was dabbling in real estate, thinking it was a straightforward way to bring home an income. A few of my triathlete colleagues, Rod, and even the kids raised the inevitable question over the next few months: "So, are you going to do an IRONMAN triathlon next?" I have to say, it was tempting to at least dream about it. If I could jump from an Olympic distance to a half-iron distance, why couldn't I jump from half-iron to full IRONMAN? Once again, there were two parts of my brain sending me conflicting messages. The doubtful one said: *You can't do that.* IRONMAN *races are for mega-athletes. It's way too much for your fragile body. You could never run the marathon portion.* But the other part of my brain was sheepishly interjecting now and then, saying: *Just maybe....*

When I attended my triathlon training group's year-end banquet in November, I sat beside my friend Jean who, at age fifty-three, had completed about seven IRONMAN races after she turned forty. I asked her the one question I had wanted to ask her for a long time: "Once you've done one IRONMAN, what keeps you going back?" Jean tried to come up with an explanation, after which she concluded: "You have to do one to understand."

Jean told me that she had registered for the 2013 IRONMAN race in Mont-Tremblant, Quebec—The Subaru IRONMAN

North American Championship. At that point, I thought: *Yes, I'm going for it. I'm signing up.* So I told Jean I was considering signing up for that race as well. She immediately responded: "It's full. It sold out in a few weeks after the 2012 race. However, there might still be some IRONMAN Foundation spots available—they are double the entry fee." This gave me the sense of urgency and momentum I needed. I was on the computer the very next day, looking to see if I could get one of the few remaining Foundation spots. To my excitement, there were some spots available. As soon as I hit the "send" button on my registration I started to panic. What was I doing? I just committed to doing an IRONMAN event! And I put $1,400 of my family's money behind it! I calmed myself with the thought that it was now or never. I was the fittest I had ever been in my life, and I didn't have a full-time job. What's more, I had an incredibly supportive husband who didn't question committing the $1,400 or my ability to complete such a ridiculously challenging event. It was definitely less difficult to swallow the steep fee knowing that $700 of it was going to the IRONMAN Foundation, which supports various athletic, community, education, health, and public benefit causes around the world.

Get the training manual out, I told myself. *You have to get serious.*

Thankfully, I would again have Rod training alongside me. He decided to sign up for the iron distance swim and cycle race in Ottawa on Labor Day weekend (my dad's birthday weekend)—part of the same event where I had done my half-iron event in 2012.

It's amazing how you're driven to get your workouts in when you've signed up for something that seems so scary and impossible to your rational brain. My first thought was that I absolutely needed to sign up for a marathon in the spring or early summer. Running a half-marathon a few months before my half-iron race definitely allowed me to believe I could finish that race. Although I felt drained getting off the bike, I could wrap my mind around doing a half-marathon by telling myself, "You've done this before." I wanted the same feeling getting off a 180 km bike ride and facing a 42.2 km marathon at the IRONMAN event. In December, not only did I sign myself up for the May 5, 2013, Mississauga Marathon, I also registered MT and gave her the receipt as her Christmas present. She laughed. She hadn't done a marathon in several years, but being the supportive friend that she is, she agreed to run it with me despite her increasingly demanding work schedule.

My January to April training schedule was more heavily weighted toward running than usual. I calculated that if I started at two hours and added ten minutes to my long run each week, I could arrive at a four hour run in twelve weeks. I needed to do my longest training run about three weeks prior to the marathon, which would mean the second week of April. My plan gave me about four weeks of wiggle room. All of my running was on a treadmill from January to March. I tend to be very nervous about slipping on wet or icy roads and sidewalks. With all the issues that have kept me from running in the past, the last thing I needed was a sprained ankle or broken leg from slipping and falling.

As the distances on the treadmill got longer, I began to feel some burning under my feet, the same type of burning I felt at the half-iron race. It usually started after about ninety minutes or so. At first I assumed it was blisters forming. My running shoes were getting old, so I replaced them with what I thought was the same Asics model I had been buying for the last seventeen years. As I started to run in the new shoes, something felt different. I could feel the burning under my feet after only about twenty minutes of running. When I went back to the store and told them about this, I was informed that the manufacturer had completely re-designed that shoe model! I couldn't believe I now had to start searching for the right running shoes a few months before my first marathon. This set off a frantic search for the right shoes. While this was going on I was also making frequent visits to the chiropractor trying to figure out the cause for the burning in my feet. Time was running out and after trying four different pairs of shoes, I made the decision to run the marathon in my old shoes even if I could feel the cushioning was worn out. I kept one new pair in which I would do some of my training runs, and I would try to spare my old shoes as much as possible so they could get me through the race.

The foot pain and shoe disaster held me back as I struggled to get my mileage up through the winter. Severe food poisoning and a family vacation to Costa Rica in March further pushed back my training. By April 5 (thirty days before the race), I was only up to two and a half hours during which I ran 22.5 km. I remember that day clearly because MT was beside me on the next treadmill. She had been sick with a stomach virus the day before and still showed up to run two and a half hours with me. Not only did she show up, she ran 27 km in the same time I ran 22.5! As exciting as it was that I had just completed my longest run ever, it was a long way from 42.2 km and time was running out. I would have to make a significant leap in time and distance on my next long run in order to get close to feeling ready for a marathon.

The following day, I participated in the annual 25 km mountain biking race I do with Rod and my brothers which involves five huge hill climbs. Despite my legs being shot from the previous day's long run, I came in second place in my age group. I had won it the year before with fresh legs, so I was very satisfied with second place. I was feeling pretty fit at this point.

Less than a week later, I was attempting a 2:45 run in order to try and catch up on mileage and get to a three-hour run by mid-April. It was April 11 and I planned to run outside for the first time since November. We got a freak ice and freezing rain storm which kept the kids home from school and left the roads much too icy for running. So I had to do yet another long run, my longest ever, on the treadmill alone in my basement.

The power of inspiring music was reinforced for me that day. I made it through two hours and forty-five minutes on a treadmill in large part thanks to my "Believe" playlist, a collection of songs selected primarily for their motivating words. Of course, I enjoy the music, but in order to make it on the "Believe" playlist, the words have to resonate. Here are some examples of inspiring lyrics from the songs on my playlist (see my complete list at the end of **Appendix II**):

The Climb—Miley Cyrus
INSPIRING LINE: *Ain't about how fast I get there, ain't about what's waiting on the other side…it's the climb.*
WHAT IT SAYS TO ME: The value of reaching for a higher goal is in the journey; whether the goal is finally reached or not is secondary.

Born This Way—Lady GaGa
INSPIRING LINE: *There ain't no other way: I was born this way.*
WHAT IT SAYS TO ME: I will make the most of what I was born with. Success is defined by how much I'm willing to challenge the limits that have been imposed upon me…maybe I'll discover that they weren't limits after all!

Marching On—the Alarm.
INSPIRING LINE: *"Our hearts must have the courage to keep on marching on."*

WHAT IT SAYS TO ME: Push through the pain and despair, no matter what. There is something better waiting for me on the other side. This song got me through a lot of mental and emotional turmoil as I was coming of age and trying to get through university.

It's My Life—Bon Jovi
INSPIRING LINE: *"It's my life and it's now or never, I ain't gonna live forever. I just want to live while I'm alive."*
WHAT IT SAYS TO ME: Do it now, do it now, do it now, and make the most of today.

My all-time most powerful motivating song is **Spirit of '76** by the Alarm because of one line: *"I will never give in, until the day that I die"*. It has helped propel me through many difficult moments. I was really hoping this song would come up near the end of this painful two hour and forty-five minute run that day. I almost fell apart when "Spirit of '76" came on three minutes before the end...I think that was my dad helping me out from above.

It was right around this time (April 2013) that I realized my purpose in life. My dreams of building a business around helping people become their own health advocates (what I now call health champions) really started to take shape when I met a brilliant marketing and social media consultant named Rebecca Mountain, owner of Impetus Social Inc. She helped me visualize how the components of such a business could come together, and it all started with telling my story by writing this book. I had an epiphany. From this point forward, my life and my work would be inextricably linked. Finishing the IRONMAN event was something I felt I now needed to do in order to draw attention to my message and help even more people. What a feeling! I soon discovered what it's like to wake up in the morning and feel great about your work. For the next few months, my work was about keeping a journal and successfully achieving a goal I couldn't even dream of four years ago. Once the IRONMAN was conquered, I would throw myself into writing a book and building a life coaching service to help others overcome limitations and reach their full potential.

But before any of that happened, I needed to prove to myself that I could complete a marathon. On April 15, 2013, about three weeks before the marathon, I was in the car on the way to picking up the kids at school when I heard about the Boston Marathon bombs on the radio. I felt sick. My friend Jean was running the Boston Marathon...oh my God! The clock at the race was around 4:09:45, which I knew would be pretty close to Jean's finishing time. When I finally reached her, she said she finished in 4:05 and was just beyond the finish line waiting for her medal when the bombs went off. What a horrible tragedy. It's hard to believe someone would have so much hatred as to kill and injure people, particularly at an event that is focused on personal accomplishment and celebrating the power of human perseverance.

This horrific event brought back the memories of September 11, 2001, just before I went to Denver for in vitro fertilization. In both cases, I concluded that we MUST carry on. We CANNOT let the evil and negative forces in this world win. I resolved to run my marathon on May 5 in defiance of the Boston terrorists. We can't run away from adversity and negative forces. We must use them as fuel to drive us toward our highest possible achievements and contributions.

On April 21 (two weeks before the marathon) I ran my longest and final training run; I ran 30 km in three hours and twenty minutes. This was the closest I had ever been to a marathon distance. I did learn that time goes by much faster when running outside, and it is much more pleasant than a treadmill.

My only issue was the horrible burning pain in the ball of my right foot. As usual, it started around the ninety-minute mark. I needed to figure out what was causing it. It went away as soon as I stopped running, so I knew it couldn't be that serious. I was in a lot of pain in the last few kilometers and really wanted to quit early. Unbelievably, my song, "Spirit of '76," came up on my iPod about two minutes before the end of my run! My playlist is on "shuffle" mode so I can't plan this! Strangely, I had had a conversation with my dad in my mind just a few minutes earlier.

As for the mileage gap between 30 km and 42.2 km, an experienced marathon runner put my mind at ease about it (sort of). She said: "After thirty kilometers, the pain is all the same to your body. It won't necessarily help you to go longer, especially if you're having foot pain issues."

With the help of Jillian, my strength coach; Carm, my chiropractor; and a few helpful friends with running experience, I was able to manage the foot pain enough to do my minimum training, but I knew there would be some significant pain involved in getting through the marathon. The best I could hope for was a relatively pain free two hours, after which I would have to be prepared to suffer in order to finish the race. I started to notice that foot massages helped quite a bit, so I used a combination of rolling a massage ball under my feet, massaging them myself, and getting Rod or my massage therapist to do it as well. I also did FSM protocols every chance I got. Could this problem be related to my chronic myofascial syndrome? The thought was beginning to cross my mind. I also started to think about how, after the Ottawa half-iron event, I had started to slack a little bit when it came to my nutrition plan and getting sufficient sleep—two important elements in ensuring optimal myofascial tissue function. While I was busy finding solutions that could get me past this latest problem of foot pain, I really needed to re-focus my efforts on all the things that got me to the half-iron distance.

On our wedding anniversary, April 25, Rod and I spent a great day together. It reinforced how lucky I am to have him in my life. He is such a great supporter. Never does he question my ability to accomplish whatever goals I set for myself. He's always there to enable my success. He helped me brainstorm possible solutions to the foot pain. I tried applying some metatarsal pads recommended by a chiropractor filling in for Carm, but when I did a short test run, my feet hurt within thirty minutes. The only good news is that they hurt in a different place!

With one week to go, I had the realization that if I waited until I felt 100 per cent to do any of these events, I would never do any of them. There's always lots of minor nagging spasms and stiffness. I've learned that I have to do what I can to get my body feeling just good enough to be able to start the race, and usually I get through it just fine. In fact I often feel much better after the race than before the start. It's just the way my soft tissues are. Based on my experience, the first question that I should ask myself is: "What needs to happen in order for me to be able to do this?" or "If I can't do it all, what part of it *can* I do?" I knew that for the next week, I needed to focus on making the soft tissues loosen up as much as possible: Chiropractor, FSM, Epsom salt baths, massage, ice, and rolling with a ball. This, along with my training and my drive to be the model of determination for my kids, would allow me to believe I could run a marathon.

Another important motivator was the desire to show the world that physical barriers can be broken. This was yet another step toward IRONMAN—a physical feat that many believe can only be achieved by superior physical specimens! By finishing an IRONMAN event (or at least attempting it), I believed I would have the experience to write my book and give others hope that they can achieve something much greater than they believe is possible.

On April 30, I started taking iron injections through Dr. Galea's office, as it became obvious that the oral supplements were not sufficient for me. Over the course of about nine months since starting high dose iron pills, my blood level had only increased from 16 to 23. I needed it to be about four times that level prior to August for the IRONMAN race.

MT and I met to discuss our marathon strategy. She claimed to be undertrained, but I knew what she was capable of. We ended up agreeing that she would run about 30 km at her own pace, then she would stop and wait for me in order to help me finish the last 12 km. During our conversation, she indicated that she wanted to contribute in some way to my book. Given that her name would be all over the story, I asked her to write the foreword. She looked surprised and honored. I thought to myself: *Does she have any idea what role she has played in helping me get to where I am?* I hope that by the time she gets to this point in the book she realizes what she has meant to me all these years. She is the sister I never had.

By May 2, all of my efforts with rolling, massaging, and FSM really seemed to be helping my feet. Things were loosening up significantly. It's amazing how simple steps can make such a difference. I was speaking to my long-time friend Fiona, who, about three years before, had had such a painful back problem that she never thought she could be physically active again. We were talking about how great it feels to be out there running, racing, setting physical goals. The difference for her (much like me) was finding someone who could help with relieving the discomfort just enough to give her a glimmer of hope that she could resume her normal life, and maybe even reach new heights in physical fitness. In 2013, Fiona ran her first-ever half marathon and continues to run and challenge herself with new physical goals. We talked about how setbacks can cause us to fear the worst and jump to negative conclusions. A few weeks before her most recent race, her back "went" again. However, knowing what works for her, she signed up for massage and chiropractic treatment (ART, acupuncture) and within a week she was running a 10 km race. Once you realize that it's not the end of the world if things don't feel 100 per cent, you become more willing to test things out. By at least testing the situation, you find out whether you really can't do the activity, or if the activity actually makes you feel better. On my last long run (30 km), I started out with some stiffness and spasm on my left side. I seriously doubted I could make it 30 km that day. However, experience has taught me that I at least have to give it a try. What's the worst that can happen?

On May 4, my kids participated in a "mud run," and each ran their longest distance to date—2 km for Sabrina and 3 km for Arquelle. They showed incredible determination and completed their runs, despite obstacles and challenges, including muddy, slippery slopes. What a great lead-in to my marathon day!

May 5 was a beautiful, sunny day with a forecasted high of 22 degrees C. I had a driver pick me up at 5:45 a.m. We then went to MT's house to pick her up and got to the race site by 6:30 a.m. Race start time was 7:30 a.m. It was still cool outside, so we tried to find a sunny spot to stand in. I ate half a protein bar and took two Tylenol and a salt pill at 7:00 a.m. We hit the porta-potties one last time around 7:15 a.m. Then it was time to enter the start corral. There was a brief moment of silence to remember the tragedy at the Boston marathon. They played *Sweet Caroline*, the song that is traditionally played at the start of the Boston race. It was pretty emotional. MT and I squeezed hands, and before we knew it, the start signal went off.

At the 9 km mark, I felt a sudden, unfamiliar pain in my right hip that shot down my leg into my foot. My right hip, glute, and quad started going into spasm. I kept telling myself it probably wasn't serious. If it were serious, the pain would be more prevalent than the spasm. By the 13 km mark, the balls of my feet (especially the right) were burning and hurting pretty badly. I stopped on the side of the road, took my shoes and socks off, and put some blister pads under my right foot. I also used the opportunity to stretch, especially my right side which was in spasm. The cushioning from the blister pads did help quite a bit, as did the stretching, so I was able to run another 6 km without stopping. Around 19 km, I had to stretch again. The pain was coming back under my feet, and my legs felt like they didn't want to move forward (especially the right). At this point, I seriously questioned how I could complete another 23 km. Despite walking a few short segments and having to stop to stretch again around 25 km, I ran most of the way from 19 km to 30 km in quite a bit of pain. My beautiful friend MT, who had run 30 km in two hours and fifty minutes, waited forty-five minutes for me to catch up to her! She then "pulled" me through the final 12 km in which I shattered my all-time distance record. During that final 12 km, I stopped a few times to stretch, but I ran most of it with MT encouraging me every step of the way. We walked a couple of hills, but I couldn't have run those any faster than I could have walked them, so why waste the energy? The last time I stopped briefly was at the 40 km mark where MT gave me an elbow to the glute muscle to help release my right side in the hopes of being able to finish as strong as possible. It helped a ton. I felt a huge release and was able to run the final 2.2 km without stopping (and with less pain in that hip and leg).

It is really hard to describe the feeling of crossing the finish line after something so punishing. Within about 50 meters of the finish line, I started to cry. They called my name; I cried harder. I crossed the finish line after five hours and seventeen minutes, feeling an incredible sense of relief and disbelief. It had been even more difficult than I had imagined. Before this, the biggest mental accomplishment of my life was that first open water swim in my very first triathlon in 2009. This marathon just moved into first place. It was five hours and seventeen minutes of mental and physical toughness I didn't know I was capable of. The open water swim in 2009 at least didn't involve pain, so it was more of a battle against fear and exhaustion. This one represented the mental toughness to push on despite the physical pain and exhaustion.

So why and how did I push myself through those difficult hours? The most important question here is "Why?" Having recovered from all those years of disability and knowing that my mission in life is to help people going through similar physical challenges, I knew that this marathon was integral to allowing me to tell a compelling story; it would show others that with enough determination, they can get out of their suboptimal physical state. That thought, combined with my desire to be a model of determination and drive for my children, is what forced me to find the *how*. The following are some of the images and thoughts I used to push me through:

✪ Terry Fox's response when someone asked him how, with all the pain from his prosthetic leg rubbing and pushing on his stump, he could run a marathon per day: "One step at a time, one telephone pole at a time, one mile at a time." How could my pain be anywhere near what Terry's pain was? In my race I kept telling myself to make it to the next telephone pole or lamppost. At the 19 km mark, when I seriously questioned whether I could finish the run, I reached back to my very first triathlon when I really didn't think I could finish the swim in Lake Ontario. How did I manage to finish that? Part of it was knowing my family was waiting for me on the shore, and the other part was the fact that passing the first buoy gave me some hope that I was moving forward, and if I could just make it to the next buoy I'd be halfway there. So I started looking for certain kilometer markers. "I have to make it to 21 km because I've run that distance several times before," I told myself, then "I have to make it to 30 km, because I've done that before and MT will be waiting.

✪ I told myself things like: "The tougher the pain, the sweeter the victory"; "It's going to hurt whether you take a break or not, so you might as well just keep going. That way it'll be over faster."

✪ I listened to my "Believe" playlist starting at the two-hour mark. I leaned on every inspiring phrase in those songs.

✪ I thought about my dad encouraging me from above.

✪ I thought about Erik Weihenmayer, a man who was visually impaired, who climbed the seven highest peaks in the world. I was reading *The Adversity Advantage* by Dr. Paul Stoltz and Erik Weihenmayer at the time of the marathon. Weihenmayer's stories of pain and struggling inspired me to remain positive about the run, despite not being able to do it in under five hours. His message is that every adversity gives us an opportunity to get better and stronger. I knew that this race would not be optimal, would involve a lot of pain, but it would help me figure out how I could be stronger for the run part of the IRONMAN. I had to use the adversity to get better and stronger. If you think about it, this mental response to adversity can be used in all parts of our lives to make us stronger and better.

✪ At the 35 km mark, with 7.2 km left, I thought about how 7 km was the distance I ran in my first triathlon. I remembered that "zoned out" feeling that came over me in the last kilometer of that run—almost a meditative state where you block everything out and just stare in the distance with nothing going through your mind. I tried to replicate that mental state as much as possible.

The bottom line is, if you can figure out a powerful enough *why*, then you will find the *how*. Unfortunately, most of us look at a really difficult goal and ask ourselves, "How could I possibly accomplish that?" The first question to ask is, "What is so important to me in my life that it would drive me to accomplish something beyond what I believe I'm capable of right now?" Overcoming thirteen years of disability and frustration is what drove me to push myself to new levels. Before thirteen years of *your* life pass by, I urge you to recognize and harness the power that you have in your current state. If everything in your life came easily, you would never be able to discover just how high you can go. It is the adversity—the difficulties—that, if utilized properly, can provide the fuel to drive us to new heights.

MT and I took a taxi back home, where my beautiful family waited to congratulate me with lots of hugs and some original artwork for my accomplishment wall. I've started putting up symbols of our family's physical accomplishments on a wall in our workout room in the basement. These include medals collected from various races, some posters made by the kids that they used to cheer us on from the sidelines, congratulatory artwork and race photos.

It was pretty tough going down the stairs the next morning. After dropping the kids off at school, I did several recovery protocols on the FSM and iced my feet by submerging them in a bucket of ice water—a new, additional strategy offered by Jillian to deal with the foot pain. I also made sure I took the maximum dose of Immunocal® (described in **Appendix II**) and ate lots of protein for the next several days. Other than the expected aches and pains after running 42.2 km, I was surprised by how good I felt and how well I was recovering. The positive, congratulatory messages I got through text message and Facebook reinforced how loved and supported I felt through the whole marathon training.

Chapter 10—Looking Back: Lessons Learned

✓ It is absolutely critical to determine your reason(s) WHY you want to accomplish something difficult and challenging. This WHY must be tied to deep and powerful emotions, which will help carry you through the most difficult moments when your logical mind tells you to walk away.

✓ Pushing through some discomfort, combined with a strong WHY, will drive you to keep searching for solutions that can make things more comfortable down the road. Keep going back to your trusted resources who have helped you in the past. Chances are they will have more helpful advice for you when you share your most recent difficulties.

✓ It is very powerful to read stories about others who overcame challenges even more difficult than yours. Reading *The Adversity Advantage* and understanding the incredible hurdles faced by a blind mountain climber conquering the seven highest peaks in the world did a lot to convince me I could get through a simple marathon.

Chapter 10—Health Champion in Action

It's All In Your Head

I met a thirty-something woman recently who told me her story of perseverance in spite of the health care system. She suffered from excruciating headaches that continued for months after having recovered from a broken jaw. She was in so much pain that she would vomit almost every day, especially when exposed to bright light. The neurologist she saw admonished her for wasting his time, as he was busy with "patients who really needed his help." The tests ordered by this doctor showed no concrete cause for the symptoms the woman described, so his approach was to ignore her plea for relief from the unbearable pain.

Despite the suffering, she persevered with full-time work, looking forward to sleeping every night when she would have relief from the pain. After asking many questions of many health professionals, she was directed to a naturopath who, after one visit, determined that it was a nerve problem and used manual therapy to give her astonishing relief from her horrific pain.

Do your own research and ask a lot of questions of many different health professionals. There is help out there, but it's not always in the most obvious places.

11

HIGHER GROUND

Having proven to myself I could complete a marathon, the focus now turned to recovering quickly and getting back into training mode for my IRONMAN event with the emphasis on bike and strength training. With the bike being my strong suit and representing nearly half the race, I needed to make sure I made the most of that part of the race. Strength training would be critical in ensuring I made it through the run without injury. I was still figuring out the pain under my feet, and a new pain was starting to surface, this time on the top of my left foot.

One of the insights that came out of completing the marathon was that I had never had any formal instruction on running technique. Running is something we all do from a young age, so we never question whether we're doing it properly. It's one thing to run a few kilometers here and there, but I was pounding out over a hundred kilometers each month. I started to think it might make sense to consult a few experts about my running technique, so I turned to Jillian and to a chiropractor at ISM who subspecializes in gait analysis for runners. I learned quite a bit from both of them and began including some running specific drills into my strength workouts. I also became even more aware of my posture and of using the right muscles while running.

It was after a hot yoga class that I gained total clarity on what my workout schedule needed to look like in order for me to be able to show up uninjured at the IRONMAN race in August. I had to do at least one yoga class and two strength workouts every week, no matter what. The next priority was two bike workouts (one short and one long), followed by two swims (one short and one long) and one run each week. This worked out to eight workouts per week, meaning that on at least one day per week I would double up (usually, I would add the yoga class to a shorter workout on the same day).

Throughout the rest of May, my aches and pains and stiffness episodes would show up in various parts of my body, seeming to work their way up and down or side to side across my body. Although I was getting concerned about the seemingly renewed symptoms of myofascial dysfunction, I had trained myself not to panic at these episodes. After all, at age forty-seven, I was asking more of my body than I ever had in my life. I assumed I was getting close to reaching my absolute physical limit. I just had to focus on all the things I knew could help me: FSM, stretching, strength workouts, rolling, yoga, Epsom salt baths, ice, chiropractor, and my nutrition plan. I also broke through the four-hour mark on my bike in May, the goal being to complete at least one six-hour bike ride prior to July 28, my targeted tapering start date. I came to the realization that the beauty of having such a challenging goal in front of me was that I could celebrate new successes, new "firsts," and new "personal bests" on a regular basis. What would happen after IRONMAN? I would need to find new goals to keep me motivated. I reflected on how grateful I was that my condition and chronic injuries had led me to the sport of triathlon. I love doing something that allows me to continually improve. Tennis in my forties would only be frustrating, because I would never be as good as I was in my twenties, unless I played three hours a day every day. And even then...

By the end of May I had figured out that the pain under my feet was almost certainly plantar fasciitis...imagine that! Something related to fascial (connective tissue) dysfunction. I also connected the dots between my right hip problem during the marathon and the right foot being the really bad one. The "side chain" fascia stretches all the way from your neck to under your foot along the entire side of the body. It was the same old problem all over again, just dressed up differently. My running had put more strain than ever on the side chains; the myofascial dysfunction was just manifesting itself as plantar fasciitis this time. At least I knew what I was dealing with.

One day, during a visit with my good friends Donna and Fiona, I decided to get very aggressive with icing, rolling a ball under my feet and calf stretching every chance I got. Thankfully they are very understanding of the physical challenges of running and humored me during their entire visit, which lasted around seven hours. Amazingly, my feet, calves, hips, and everything up the sides of my body started to feel much better afterward. Donna passed along all the advice she got about plantar fasciitis from her chiropractor, and I started to feel confident I could beat this problem in time for August 18.

Although I was staying pretty much on track with the strength, yoga, swim, and bike portions of my workout plan, it took me until June 3 to muster up the courage to take on my first significant run after the marathon. As part of a "brick" workout (bike followed by run), I did a forty-minute run, which seemed to feel okay. On June 7, I tried my first "long" run, targeting one and a half hours to test out my feet. I was only able to do one hour and fifteen minutes. My feet were okay until about the one-hour mark, but the last fifteen minutes were pretty painful. I had not been getting much sleep that week and felt totally exhausted and demoralized after this failed long run attempt.

How could I possibly run 42.2 km to complete the IRONMAN race? Interesting how I tend to be much more fatalistic when I'm exhausted. I did lots of icing, FSM, and some rolling before going to bed that night.

The next morning, my foot and hip didn't feel as bad, which was somewhat encouraging. I continued to ice my feet on and off by submerging them in a bucket filled with ice and cold water. This was very uncomfortable, but many of the things that have helped me the most have been uncomfortable at first. I was realizing more and more that I also needed to do more rolling along the outside of the leg, from foot to hip. I also called Carm to get treatment first thing the next day. I was really feeling the urgency to get my foot problem resolved before August 18. Maybe I needed to do shorter more intense runs in order to spare my feet for the one long run that would really matter. It was so hard to know what the right strategy was.

Over the next few weeks I added some extra yoga classes in lieu of some swim or bike workouts. During one of these yoga classes, I thought about how my body felt six years earlier when I first started doing hot yoga, before my breakthrough with Jillian. Everything was so tight back then, and it was so difficult to get into many poses. I realized how far I had come, and I couldn't let this hip and foot setback get me down. How many times in the past did I feel horrible before a race and eventually worked everything out? Even with this problem, I was SO much better off than I was five or six years earlier. All I could do was focus on doing everything in my power to deal with the problem and continue to train as much as possible, especially on swim and bike. No matter what the result of my IRONMAN attempt, my life was so much more rewarding and fulfilling than it had ever been. It truly is about "the climb" and not arriving somewhere. There is no arrival point. We just keep striving to get better.

Rod had the helpful suggestion that we should get our bikes professionally fitted in order to ensure the most comfort possible in our upcoming 180 km IRONMAN bike rides. So in early June, we spent an entire day with Scott Judges at Fitt 1st, getting our bikes properly fitted to our bodies. I had no idea that having a properly fitting bike for maximum comfort, injury prevention, and pedaling efficiency could be so scientific. Scott moved my seat forward 2 cm and installed narrower handlebars, which he also moved forward 3 cm. He also placed a wedge under one shoe after he discovered that my left foot was significantly more everted (rotated outward) than the right. Another thing he noticed as part of his biomechanical analysis was that there was a significant forward rotation of my left hip, and my right shoulder was rolled down and forward. It brought back what Barbara, the physiotherapist in Cincinnati, had pointed out: that I was "crooked" and that I needed to use my core muscles to compensate. I also connected Scott's observation with my osteopath's recent comment about my being "too anterior" or rolled inward. It all fit together. So after my visit with Scott, I tried to focus on pulling my left hip and right shoulder back while cycling and running, as well as any time I thought of it during the day. I was taking in every possible clue about what could be contributing to my discomfort and implementing all possible solutions.

While attending the C3 June fundraising dinner in support of the promising young elite triathletes we had the privilege of training with, I was fortunate enough to sit with Brooke Brown, one of Canada's top female full distance triathletes. I told her I had signed up for the August 18 Subaru IRONMAN North American Championship Mont Tremblant, but was a little concerned about my ability to run, given the latest problems with my feet. She recommended getting a floating belt and substituting "water running" for some running workouts;

this would allow me to still use the running muscles without pounding on my feet. Sean Bechtel, another of Canada's best triathletes, had also suggested this to me. If these two incredible athletes recommended it, I was going to buy myself a water belt and begin doing some water running immediately. Now I had a bike that fit me better and a plan to get through the run training. My hopes were up again. The importance of affiliating with inspiring people who are doing what you want to do, but at a higher level, was becoming obvious to me.

One of our preparatory races was going to be the June 16 100 km Centurion bike race in hilly Horseshoe Valley, about an hour drive from our house. This was a perfect warm-up for my anticipated 180 km in the rolling hills of Mont-Tremblant. Rod and I got up at 4:30 a.m. that morning and headed to Horseshoe Valley in the pouring rain. We arrived to find a parking lot that was pure mud. The rain was falling so hard it was difficult to see, and there was a lot of water on the roads. Since I rarely ride in the rain (certainly never in this type of downpour), thinking of going downhill with skinny tires and less than optimal breaking ability on an unfamiliar course in the pouring rain made me very nervous. I was also exhausted, having had about four hours of sleep per night the previous two nights. I decided to play it safe and stay in the car instead of doing the race. I had my FSM machine and my massage ball with me, so I rolled my feet, did several FSM protocols, and had a nap. So much for the 100 km training ride with hills, which I badly needed to prepare for Mont-Tremblant. That being said, I'd rather be alive and show up at the race undertrained than to watch it from a hospital bed.

Rod, on the other hand, decided to participate in the race. At around 10 a.m. I received a phone call from him. He was in an ambulance heading for the hospital in Barrie, about thirty minutes away. He had crashed and been thrown from his bike, landing on his neck and head. He said he was okay and the hospital visit was precautionary. When I saw him, I could tell he was shaken up and his neck hurt. What wasn't apparent yet was the big bump on his head, which appeared later in the day. When we talked later and I looked at his cracked helmet, I realized just how bad of a crash he'd had, and how lucky we were that he didn't have any serious injuries. We talked about the value of life and the importance of not taking unnecessary risks. He was going too fast for such a wet road, and he had moved into the left lane (breaking the race rules). The biggest thing that saved him was veering off into the grass before being thrown from the bike.

Rod's crash was the first in a string of "bad luck" events to happen over the next four days. The second happened on the morning of June 18 when I finally got to the quarry for my first open water training swim of the season. I got into the water at 6:30 a.m. with the intention of doing two laps or 2,000 m. However, my ability to see the buoys and orient myself are not the greatest... something I continue to work on. I took a wrong turn at one of the buoys and ended up cutting about a quarter off of my first lap. Since the quarry gates get locked at 7:30, I added some distance to my partial loop and only completed about 1,400 m in forty minutes. *Oh well*, I thought, *it's better than nothing*. When I walked back to my car I noticed that the ground was very wet and sticky. As I tried to turn my car around to leave the quarry area, my tires got stuck in the mud. My front tires were spinning in about 10 inches of mud, and the muck was flying everywhere. The only people left at the quarry were two superstar triathletes who are part of the C3 high performance team—Sean Bechtel and Taylor Reid. They didn't give a second thought to helping me try to get out, going as far as digging mud with their bare hands. They just about had me out when my car ran out of gas! I said to them, "I should have just gone to the pool!" To which Taylor replied, "No, because then you wouldn't have a story to tell!" Wow, what a window into that athlete's mind. Another reason I love being associated with these high-level athletes.

To round out the string of bad luck events, my car was rear-ended on June 20, the day we were leaving for our family vacation to Spain. Luckily there was no major damage and the other driver agreed to cover the repairs since it was her fault. Maybe this short period of bad luck was a good thing, as our fortunes seemed to reverse themselves starting on that day. We had a fantastic trip to the south of Spain, visiting Costa del Sol and Mallorca. Aside from a few funny stories about getting lost and using our broken Spanish for directions, everything went about as smoothly as you can expect for twelve days in a foreign country with two young kids.

We had been very hopeful about doing several ocean swims to get ahead with our open water swimming. Early in the vacation, Rod and I attempted our first Mediterranean open water swim in front of the resort in Marbella. There were buoys set up from the beach, out to around 150 m, outlining a channel for boats to come in close to shore. We agreed to swim back and forth to the green buoy about 100 m from shore, hoping to do at least 1,000 m that morning. The water was freezing cold. My hands hurt from the cold after the second lap out and back. We agreed to do one or two more rounds before heading for the pool and warmer water. Rod was ahead of me and had just made his way around the green buoy as I was approaching it. Just then, I felt and heard a huge *whoosh* under me, sort of like a torpedo. I had a flashback to the time in the quarry when a group of elite swimmers literally swam over me. For a split second, I thought it was Rod passing under me, but I looked up and saw him ahead of me. Oh crap! That must have been a very large fish! I yelled out to Rod: "I felt something really big swim under me!" At that point, we started swimming as fast as we could toward shore. I had to focus on swimming, not on what might be in the water, so that I wouldn't run out of breath from panic. We finished the workout in the pool, for a total of about an hour of swimming. I didn't care whether that was a harmful fish or not, the experience put a very quick end to our dream of several open water swims in the Mediterranean ocean. Although not ideal (it was a bit short), there was a heated pool that we were able to use for several swimming workouts.

Running is always the easiest to do on vacation, but I had to be careful with my foot issues. I did a few runs, which I complemented with the elliptical trainer at the hotel gym. I also did a few strength workouts with Rod. In Mallorca, we had arranged to rent a beautiful road bike, which we had delivered to our hotel. We were both psyched about riding in Mallorca, known to be a training place for professional cycling teams. Since we would not feel comfortable leaving the girls alone for an extended period, we had to take turns using the bike. Rod picked up a cycling map and lots of good information from a bike rental shop. He mapped out a route through the mountains, including some famous climbs that the professional cyclists use for training on the island.

The next day Rod headed out at 6 a.m. for what he thought would be a four or five hour ride. He texted a couple of times along the way, describing his awesome and challenging climbs, and the beautiful scenery he was experiencing. After I responded to his second text, I saw a whole bunch of scrambled text messages coming through in quick succession. It looked as though his phone was being banged around and accidentally sending texts...my mind immediately turned to his accident a few weeks ago, and I started to panic a bit. I was visualizing him tumbling down a cliff by the side of the road. I had to stop myself several times from thinking the worst. I knew it could also just be his phone bumping around in his pocket. As it turns out, it was the latter. A few hours later, I got a great text describing an awesome 8 km classic Mallorcan climb. I was so jealous! I looked forward to my turn the next day.

While Rod was on his ride, I did leave the girls in the room for thirty minutes while I did a run along the boardwalk in Palma de Mallorca. I went at a slightly faster pace than usual and worked really hard on my posture and running form. I felt a few tweaks and pangs here and there, but overall it was a pretty good run along the Mediterranean.

That night during dinner in Palma, Rod described his seven and a half hour epic ride in much detail and took me through the map, explaining all the potential pitfalls and what to watch out for to make my ride a bit more efficient than his. Throughout all this, my brain started to go through all the "what-ifs." I started envisioning myself on the switchbacks up and down the mountain, some of which had no guardrails, and I became really worried. But I kept trying to gather up the courage. *This is once in a lifetime, and I'm training for an* IRONMAN...*I have to put the miles in.* I also knew that Mont-Tremblant would be hilly so this would be a perfect training ride...the views would be a bonus.

I woke up at 5 a.m. to experience my own epic Mallorcan bike ride. As I was getting ready I tried to visualize myself doing the ride successfully, but I just got more and more afraid. If only the kids were older and Rod and I could have rented two bikes and done some rides together. I just didn't feel confident about it. I told Rod, and he supported me (as always). I told myself: *All I need is a good hard workout, and I can see the island with the family instead of on the bike. If I use the exercise bike in the hotel from 6 to 9 a.m., I can still get a good workout and be at the room in time for a full day of fun with the family.* I went down to the hotel gym, only to find out it didn't open until 9 a.m. Curse Europe: beautiful to visit but very frustrating when it comes to the practical aspects of our lives that we take for granted in North America...like gyms opening by 6 a.m. on weekdays. Yes, I was frustrated, but I thought I did a pretty good job controlling it since it was my decision to not ride by myself. I reflected on how blessed I was to have everything I have, including my health, which was good enough to allow me to *believe* I could do a five hour ride in the mountains! I told myself that I would catch up when I got home. As with all my races, I wouldn't be as trained as I'd like to be, but that is something I have had to accept with this body of mine anyway. I reminded myself that I had consciously made the choice to take this vacation at this time of the year, and that I needed to focus on the positives.

On my first day back home from our Spanish vacation, I did my first five-hour bike ride on my own on familiar Ontario roads. The last two hours were painful, especially in the right foot and hip—the old fascial side chain issue again. Since I had not done any yoga on vacation, I did some extra classes during that first week back. I was also facing a half-iron race in Peterborough, part of my IRONMAN race preparation, four days after returning from Spain. I really wasn't confident about the run part, as my longest run since the marathon had been only about 12 km. The half-iron distance involves a 21.1 km run after the 1.9 km swim and 90 km bike ride. I was getting used to that "unprepared" feeling before races. My thought going in was: *Do a good swim, a strong bike, and the run may or may not happen.* Rod and I went together to Peterborough, where he completed the half-iron distance swim and bike event, and I was able to complete the half-iron triathlon one minute faster than my 2012 Ottawa event! Both Carm's recommendation to place pads in specific places inside my shoes and the discovery that my feet felt better when I massaged my shins, got me through the run with much less pain than I expected. It's all about searching and discovering all the time. I was beginning to learn that the more questions I ask, the more solutions I discover and the more I can accomplish.

As part of my continued search and discovery mission to fix my body, I tend to search online for new information on my condition on a semi-regular basis. With time running out and my confidence still shaky about my ability to complete the IRONMAN event on August 18, I turned to the internet where I found a very interesting article about chronic myofascial pain syndrome. Just when I thought I had learned everything I could about managing the condition, I picked up additional information from this article. One of the insights was on the effectiveness of trigger point injections. There was evidence that injections directly into trigger points could help release the areas within the muscle where overstimulated contraction cells (sarcomeres) become unable to release from contraction. Most of us would refer to these as "knots" in the muscle and almost everyone has experienced a muscle knot at some point, but those of us with chronic myofascial pain syndrome are riddled with trigger points and we can never totally get rid of them.

Armed with this new knowledge, I went to see Dr. Galea to inquire about whether trigger point injections were an option for me. He noted that I have so many trigger points (potentially hundreds) that it would be difficult to do injections. As an alternative to targeted injections, he suggested intravenous (IV) infusions of electrolytes to heavily hydrate the tissues. He felt that this should greatly reduce the trigger point activity by enabling better functioning of the fascia. If there were a few key active trigger points remaining, he could inject those in the next couple of weeks. I really hoped this could help. What was reinforced for me during this interaction with Dr. Galea was that health professionals will not come and find you to offer solutions, but if they're good, they will have some answers to your questions. So you *must* do your research and ask questions.

I had a disastrous bike workout on July 12. I was supposed to do a five-hour bike ride, which I thankfully decided to do in the basement on the trainer. My bike shorts were uncomfortable, so I stopped to change them. My seat felt like it was too far forward, so I stopped to adjust it back. My legs were tired, my feet hurt, and I felt stiff. I gave up after two and a half hours and spent forty-five minutes stretching. It felt like I was regressing instead of making progress in my training. Just over a month to go before Mont-Tremblant. Was it time to panic yet?

You'd think I would have known not to panic by this point. I can think of countless occasions when a really bad day was followed by a good day. A few days after the disastrous bike ride attempt of July 12, I had a fantastic 110 km ride in the hills of Caledon that I completed in four-and-a-half hours. Although my feet started to hurt toward the end of the ride, it was a big confidence booster. This was also the day that I went for my first IV infusion of electrolytes. During my drive home from the IV session, I started to feel a lot of relief from the stiffness in various parts of my body. I thought maybe I was imagining things—perhaps a placebo effect. When I woke up the next morning, I couldn't believe the amount of release in my muscles and connective tissues. I felt like my body was lengthening. I started to see a glimmer of hope again...maybe I could run the marathon part of the IRONMAN event.

I proceeded to have three more IV infusions over the next ten days. My body was feeling good and I started breaking up my run workouts into three parts: elliptical trainer, water running, and outdoor running. It was good variety and helped me get in the mileage with less pain and discomfort.

On July 24, I swam three laps of the quarry (3,000 m) for the first time that year (I had only done it once the previous year). I was behind schedule on my long open water swims and was feeling a sense of urgency, if not panic, about being grossly undertrained. After one and a half laps of the quarry, I started cramping and came close to quitting. Every time I moved my legs and tried to kick, the cramping would get worse. But I told myself: *Imagine you're in the middle of your swim at Tremblant. You can't quit. You have to continue. Whatever it takes to complete the third lap.* So I started to rely more on my arms in order to drag my legs along. The crazy thing is that I passed one guy at the end of my second lap when I felt like I was barely moving. Granted, he was really slow, but I thought to myself: *Yay, I'm passing someone! I don't care if he's injured and eighty years old...I'm passing him!* That kept me going for a while and even put a little bit more energy into my third lap. I also thought about why I was training for this IRONMAN race. I had to be able to complete it. It was the culmination of my story that is meant to inspire and help a lot of people to overcome health issues and reach higher.

By July 25, I hadn't decided which pair of running shoes I would wear in Tremblant. I was still comparing three different pairs. The old ones I wore for the marathon were definitely out, since they were much too worn. I finally decided on a pair of Sauconys; they felt like they had the most cushion and had more room in the toe box for me to stretch out my toes.

How much adversity must I face in preparing for this race? On July 27, during what was supposed to be my first ever six-hour bike ride, I felt a pain in my left calf at the four-hour mark. After stretching it out I was able to continue for another hour at a much lower resistance, but didn't achieve my goal for that training session. Yikes, I was supposed to be doing my longest training run the next day: three hours. That night, between FSM, stretching, rolling, and icing sessions, I read a few more pages of *The Adversity Advantage* by Dr. Paul Stoltz and Erik Weihenmayer. It was just what I needed to strengthen my resolve to persevere through whatever obstacles are thrown at me. I would succeed with completing the IRONMAN race somehow and this would allow me to make a difference in people's lives in the long term.

My calf didn't feel too bad the next day, so I did one-and-a-half hours of my run training on the elliptical trainer followed by one hour and fifteen minutes outside. I got through it without aggravating things too much on the left side. I started to wonder if my decision to move my bike seat back a few weeks ago could be contributing to this calf problem. I scheduled a follow up meeting with the bike fitter the following week. I was really cutting it close with less than three weeks to go before my big race.

I think the better my nutrition and hydration, the better all the techniques like yoga, rolling, and FSM are allowed to work. Years ago, when I didn't understand the role of nutrition, supplements, and hydration, I would stretch and roll for hours to get minor relief that would last only minutes, then everything would go back to being "bunched up" and tight. With the IV sessions added on to my nutrition and supplement plan, I seemed to be recovering from issues like the calf incident rather quickly using stretching, yoga, rolling, etc.

As Dr. Galea had suggested, the IV sessions cleared up a lot of stiffness and trigger points. It felt like there were four key trigger points remaining, and all seemed related to the initial muscle tear in my left hip from 1996: two in the hip, one in the

IT band, and one in the calf. He injected all four sites with vitamin B12. As I was driving home from the appointment, I could feel some incredible release happening along the left side, from hip to calf. Wow. I had to call Rod and tell him. One more step in the right direction, but was it too close to race day? When trigger points that have been knotted up for many years are released, instability in surrounding muscles could be revealed. I was counting on all my hard work with strength training paying off. I hoped that my muscles would be strong enough to handle the trigger point releases. The ideal would have been to release the trigger points and then strengthen the newly relaxed muscles. But no situation is ever ideal. All I could hope for was that it would all come together the right way.

Up to this point, my longest swim ever had been 3,000 meters. I had to know that I could swim 4,000 m in open water, so on July 31 I did four laps of the quarry for the first time. It started to rain after my first lap. I prayed for no lightning, as they would call us out of the water at the first sign of lightning. *I've left this way too late. What if I can't complete the swim today?* Luckily, no lightning was seen and I completed my four laps in two hours as I expected. There were several moments when I felt a cramp coming on, but I was able to keep it at bay by relaxing my legs. Barrie Shepley (former Olympic coach, international triathlon commentator, and head of the C3 training organization) was on lifeguard duty on the paddleboard and was nice enough to check on me and encourage me during the last lap. Drained but so proud and satisfied, I stumbled out of the quarry to learn that I had actually done 4,200 m in two hours. The IRONMAN swim is 3,800 M, so I calculated that I should be able to do it in around 1:45 or 1:50, with more than thirty minutes to spare before the cut-off time of two hours and twenty minutes.

During my appointment with Scott, the bike fitter, he informed me that moving my seat back a few centimeters as I had done resulted in an effective increase in seat height of 2.5 cm. This was significant enough to overstretch my hamstrings and calves. He put the seat back to where it was previously but angled the handlebars in a way that would allow me to stretch forward a bit more. My last window of opportunity for a six-hour bike ride was coming up in a few days. A one-and-a-half hour test ride felt okay immediately after Scott's readjustment. On August 3, Rod and I completed a six-hour bike ride in which we covered 140 km. Rod wondered if that was enough, given the 180 km ride I was facing in Mont-Tremblant. My response: "I went 140 km without any significant calf or other pain. That will have to do."

The next day, I felt compelled to repeat the 4,200 m quarry swim. This would be exactly two weeks prior to Mont-Tremblant. I would complete this last long swim, then it would be two weeks of tapering that would include lots of yoga, easy strength workouts, and cutting back significantly on bike, swim, and run distances. At the quarry, it was windy and the water was surprisingly choppy for such a small body of water. One side of the quarry wasn't bad, but when I got toward the back and turned the first corner, it felt like I was in the ocean being slapped around by whitecaps. It was brutal. I was swallowing tons of water and trying not to inhale any! I was pretty determined and felt strong on my first lap, so I tried not to let the waves distract me. I focused on getting into a rhythm and plowing through the rough waters. I was feeling a bit panicky when I hit the big waves again on my second lap, but I just kept on pushing. Near the end of the third lap, I got some pretty bad cramps and almost talked myself into quitting before thinking to myself: *This is the last time you have to do this distance before Mont-Tremblant. If you quit now, you'll have to try again in a few days...just get it over with!* So I persevered, just dragging my legs behind me to avoid severe cramping. My time was slow—2:07—but it would have been well under the 2:20 cut-off for 3,800 m at Tremblant. I desperately hoped I wouldn't have to face such turbulent waters for the race. I was so disoriented and shivering when I got out of the water, it was a real challenge to pull off my wetsuit. When we got home, I jumped into the hot tub (with Epsom salts) and stayed there for quite a while. My wonderful husband took care of dinner (despite the fact that he had also just swam 4,200 m with me). Now I knew for sure I would make it through 3,800 m at Mont-Tremblant. To think that a few years ago it was the swim that I feared the most in long distance triathlons.

My last few swim, bike, and run workouts between August 5 and 14 were confidence builders. I was so undertrained on the run that I needed to focus on it, yet I had to be careful to not overdo the training during that last crucial week. I decided to do a two-hour combination of elliptical and running. After thirty good minutes on the elliptical trainer, I went out for a one-and-a-half-hour run. It turned out to be my best run since January. There were some aches and pains, but they were quite manageable. At that moment, I actually believed I was ready to do the IRONMAN. Bring it on!

Until I woke up the next morning with tightness in my left hip. And the roller coaster ride continued. I told myself there was nothing to worry about, just the same old stuff. My friend Jean (who was also doing the Mont-Tremblant event) put my mind at ease by telling me that she always felt some weird aches and pains during the taper phase.

The other reassuring thing that happened during these last few training days was my mom telling me that I should stop and not complete the race at the first sign of pain. Being the rebel that I am, I welcomed this advice from my mom. Now I was more determined than ever to complete the race, no matter what!

As I read the IRONMAN race materials on August 12, I discovered that I had to pick up my race kit in Mont-Tremblant before 4 p.m. on August 16 in order to be allowed at the start line. We had planned to leave the morning of the sixteenth and it was at least an eight-hour drive. There was no way I could take the chance of getting caught in traffic or encountering some other sort of delay and missing my opportunity to participate in the race. We had to leave on the fifteenth. I quickly booked a cheap hotel for the night of August 15 in Cornwall, a little more than half way to Mont-Tremblant. I had the morning of August 15 booked with three final health care appointments, so we would leave late in the afternoon. After my IV, chiropractic treatment, and additional trigger point injections, I felt pretty good the rest of the day. The drive to Cornwall was brutally slow, the highway jammed with construction for miles on end. We didn't get to the hotel in Cornwall until 1 a.m. After a few hours of poor quality sleep, we were back on the road by 9 a.m. wanting to make sure we got to Tremblant well before the 4 p.m. cut off to pick up my race kit.

We arrived in the beautiful ski village of Mont-Tremblant at 1 p.m., at which time I immediately lined up for the race kit pick-up. It was a thirty-minute wait to get in, but once inside, the process was extremely well organized. There was waiver signing, a weigh-in, and the all-important pick up of the race kit that included my race numbers, the timing chip, and detailed instructions about dropping off my bike and transition bags the next day. As I looked around at all the fit athletes,

I still couldn't believe I was among them. By now, I considered myself a reasonably experienced triathlete, but I was in a whole new league here. I had to keep shutting down that annoying voice in my head that kept trying to say: "You don't belong here. This is way above your head."

That night, I smashed my ankle against a metal bed post at the hotel. It hurt so much it drew tears, and I was frozen for a few minutes thinking I had done some real damage. Thankfully, there was only a small cut and bruise, and I did not feel anything with walking. This always seemed to happen to me before races. I remembered that the night before my very first triathlon, I walked into a door frame and smashed my shoulder really hard. I made it through that first race though, so I thought maybe this ankle incident could be a good omen!

The day before the race was filled with organizing my gear, preparing drink bottles, filling up my transition bags, dropping off my bike, rolling, stretching, and doing some easy activation exercises to keep the muscles loose and mobile. I also spent time relaxing on the beach and watching the kids play in the water. Dropping off my bike and transition bags was a moving experience. As I approached the transition area, I saw a sea of bikes set against the Laurentian mountains and the pretty village of Mont Tremblant. For a fleeting moment, I thought about how much easier it would be to just walk away...to not even show up to start this huge challenge the next day. I had to quickly shut down that line of thinking. These are the thoughts we can't allow to win when facing any challenge. Facing an IRONMAN race is just a simulation, a practice run, for all the real challenges we need to confront in our lives.

That night, I remembered how massaging my shins helped me get through the Peterborough half-iron race. I asked Rod to massage my lower legs, where I felt a lot of tension. It felt amazing. I finished off with rolling up and down the sides of my legs, focusing on the outer calf area, which seemed to loosen everything up.

Before bed, after Sabrina had gone to sleep, Arquelle helped me place my race number and age stickers on my arm and calf, respectively. It was great to have her feel part of the experience. Everyone was in bed by 9:30 p.m. with alarms set for 3:30 a.m.

As I lay in bed trying not to think too much about what was ahead of me the next day, I could feel tightness releasing from calves to shoulders. Great timing! Then something strange happened. As was the case four years earlier, the night before my very first triathlon, I felt something on my leg (again, the leg on the side of the bed where Rod wasn't). For a second, I thought there was a small animal on the bed or that one of the kids was there. It startled me. But there was nothing on the bed and no one else in the room. It had to be my dad. I was dedicating this race to him and to my beautiful girlfriends who had lost their dads: Jodi, Stacey, and most recently Donna whose dad had passed away three days before I left for Mont-Tremblant. It made me so sad not to be there to support her at the funeral the way she had been there when I lost my dad. But knowing Donna, I was confident that she was pulling for me and would never hold it against me. I eventually drifted off to sleep, thinking about the fact that I could already claim my victory. My win happened the day I came to believe I could complete an IRONMAN triathlon. Showing up and doing the race was the icing on the cake.

Chapter 11—Looking Back: Lessons Learned

✓ Being strong and healthy is a process, not a place where you arrive. Constant vigilance and effort is required, but the outcome is so rewarding.

✓ Setbacks are to be expected. This expectation prevents unnecessary panic and frustration at the first sign of a problem rearing its ugly head.

✓ Even if you think you've gotten as far as you can in terms of health improvement, keep an open mind, stay on the lookout for additional solutions, and keep asking questions.

✓ Many health problems need to be addressed from various perspectives. You'll arrive at feeling better after many small steps are taken. It's unlikely that there will be only one "magic bullet." While I'm still working on getting to a better state, I made huge progress over four years after addressing a number of issues that I discovered over time. Some of the effective solutions for me were:

  ✪ Nutrition and supplements to reduce inflammation and improve the tissue repair process
  ✪ Strength and flexibility training
  ✪ Effective use of the roller and ball to work out trigger points and stimulate the fascia
  ✪ Treating sleep apnea to allow better tissue repair
  ✪ Maximizing hydration, including occasional IV treatments to ensure sufficient electrolytes for optimal connective tissue function
  ✪ Trigger point injections to release knots in the muscles

✪ Occasional visits to the chiropractor, massage therapist, and osteopath to address any developing problems before they become widespread

✓ No matter how much you trust and respect your health professional and his/her solutions, you are still the ultimate decision maker when it comes to:

 ✪ Whether you will attempt to implement the solution in the first place; and
 ✪ Whether you will consistently persevere with implementing the solution to obtain the full benefit. You have to ask yourself: Does it fit within your lifestyle? Are you willing to change your lifestyle to gain the benefit of this solution?

✓ When you do something challenging like a race or a competition that is a stretch for you, it's important to look at it as an opportunity to uncover your weaknesses so that you can take appropriate steps to work on these afterward. The marathon was critical in bringing out issues that I had to address before the IRONMAN. When I played tennis, tournaments would cause me a lot of stress and frustration but I always appreciated the fact that my weaknesses were highlighted to me during matches, and I could do some specific training on those weaknesses. These issues might not have become obvious had I not signed up for the competition (and lost).

✓ Find individuals or groups of people who are achieving what you want to achieve. Spend as much time as you can with them, follow them on social media, and do whatever you need to do to be influenced by them. Immerse yourself with positive influences.

Chapter 11—Health Champion in Action

Overcoming Multiple Sclerosis
(Story taken with permission from the book:
Inspire Me Well by Lisa Bélanger and Sarah O'Hara)

When Crystal Phillips, a competitive speed skater, was diagnosed with multiple sclerosis at the peak of her skating career, her doctors told her it was in her best interest to never skate again. Exercises as strenuous as speed skating, they told her, would only exacerbate the symptoms of her disease. Crystal felt that she knew her body best and decided to do her own research and make some key lifestyle changes to minimize the symptoms of her condition.

Although doctor after doctor told her that she shouldn't be physically active, she knew that the right amount of exercise actually improved how she felt. So she gradually began skating again, experimenting with the "right" amount that would make her feel better, not worse. She made changes to her nutrition, eliminating any artificial components in her food, and also took high quality supplements. Over time, her skating improved and her symptoms lessened. Ultimately, she was the driver behind her treatment plan. Having launched her own charities to raise awareness and funding for MS and all neurological diseases, Crystal believes she was blessed to have been dealt this life challenge that, with the right mindset, turned into an opportunity to make a difference and to inspire others to overcome obstacles to reach whatever dreams they may have.

My conclusion from this story is that taking control is the key when you're faced with health challenges. You cannot achieve your best possible outcome unless you are the director of your own health improvement program.

12

THE IMPOSSIBLE BECOMES POSSIBLE: AUGUST 18—RACE DAY

I was up with the first beep of the alarm clock at 3:30 a.m. I immediately started going through my morning race routine: rolling, activation exercises, lots of hydration, breakfast #1 (I would eat again in the transition area before the start of the race). It took some effort to get the kids up, but they were excited enough for me that it didn't take as much as I thought. We piled into the car to arrive at the race site by 4:40 a.m., early enough to get a good parking spot.

Rod walked me to the transition area as the kids stayed and rested in the car. He said to me: "I have to believe this is the most nervous you've ever been before a race." I answered, "Maybe, but I'm trying to block it out." When I think about it now, I was strangely not nervous. I really felt like I couldn't lose. Just showing up was amazing. And my body felt pretty good, so I was reasonably confident I could not only finish, but come in under fifteen hours. It was a strange experience because I kept thinking that I should be nervous. Whenever I would let myself "feel the moment," the emotions were not so much those of anxiety or nervousness, but rather those of the relief and elation I imagined I would feel upon crossing the finish line.

After a good luck kiss and hug from Rod, I entered the transition area around 5 a.m. The 2,600 bikes were set up on racks outside, and there was a huge white tent the size of a football field inside which were all the transition bags, organized by transition number (#1 swim-to-bike and #2 bike-to-run) and by athlete bib number.

There were also curtained changing areas for athletes who wanted to change clothes between events.

I soaked in the atmosphere for a moment and then found a corner in which to do some last minute stretching and rolling (yes, I brought my massage ball with me). Just before 6 a.m. I put my wetsuit on halfway and started the ten-minute walk to the beach. I noticed some pain in my left foot while walking in the sand. Rather than dwell on this new twinge, I decided to take in all that was going on around me. The beach was packed with thousands of athletes and spectators. There were air force jets saluting us, and helicopters capturing TV footage. It was surreal. What was I doing there?

The swim felt fantastic. The water was calm and not too cold. I just did my thing, knowing I wouldn't be fast but also confident I would make it well under the cut-off time as long as I just kept swimming. There were more lifeguards than I had ever seen at a triathlon, which helped me feel calm and safe. In addition, I was almost at the very back, so I didn't have the pressure of people coming up behind me and passing me. As I rounded the first turn, I figured I had completed about 1,700 meters and was feeling great about it. I was not tired at all. About then, I started to feel a bit of spasm in the left side of my back (probably not a coincidence it was the same side as the foot pain I had felt on the beach), but I just kept thinking it was nothing. *Just relax and it will go away.*

I did get hit in the feet a few times, and one woman criss-crossed in front of me three times. I did my share of damage by accidentally hitting one woman right in the crotch! Aside from these few minor incidents, the 3,800 meters were mostly smooth and uneventful.

Coming out of the water, I checked my watch, and it looked like I came out after one hour and fifty-one minutes, almost exactly what I had anticipated. Rod and the girls were there to cheer me on. I felt great. There were volunteers there to pull wetsuits off. This was a first for me: a welcome treat. No struggling with weak arms and hands to try to pull it off myself. This was followed by a pretty long run up to the transition. In the past, I'd mostly walked this part of the race; I worried about screwing something up by running in bare feet. This time, I started running and everything felt pretty good, so I ran all the way to transition.

The transition area was a new experience as well. There were so many amazing volunteers ready to help with anything I needed. I was prepared to take my time and have a slow transition to psyche myself for the bike, but the volunteers were so efficient that I felt the need to get out of there fast so as not to disappoint them. As I came out of the transition tent, a volunteer guided me to my bike and helped me take it off the rack. My heart sank a little when I didn't see Rod and the kids, but I realized how much of an effort it would have been for them to pack up all their gear and walk from the beach to the transition area.

Just before taking my bike from the volunteer, I popped some Tylenol, Traumeel tablets (a homeopathic anti-inflammatory I had recently discovered), and a salt pill into my mouth. I doubled up on the Traumeel thinking it was harmless. In retrospect, I think it really irritated my stomach. The first two hours on the bike I had something that felt like a combination of a stitch, cramp, and spasm in my right side. I felt like I needed to have a bowel movement. In terms of pace though, I had a great start to the ride, averaging almost 30 km/h. I started passing people and kept track of the number to keep my mind occupied. Just as I was thinking I might be able to complete the bike segment in six-and-a-half hours and not the seven hours for which I had prepared myself, the wind picked up and it became really difficult to keep up the speed. My heart rate dropped as my legs got heavy and I couldn't push as hard as my heart was capable of handling. My lower back started to hurt. By five hours, I felt that foot pain I had felt on the beach that morning. Then the pain went up my lower leg to the upper calf. I arched my back up and down in "cat and cow" yoga poses while riding to keep things stretched out as much as possible. I also focused a lot on my posture, pulling the left hip and right shoulder back, which seemed to help somewhat.

The stomach upset made it hard to take salt pills, which caused me some concern about the risk of cramping. Thankfully the temperature was not too hot so the amount of sweating was within reasonable limits, thus reducing the quantity of salt supplementation needed. The thought of eating the stuff in my snack pouch made me nauseated. How was I going to keep up my energy? Luckily, the aid stations had Honey Stinger Waffles that seemed appealing, so I took a few. They were easy to keep down and even settled my stomach. After that discovery (around the three-hour mark), I was able to start taking salt pills and eating more. I ended up making four necessary porta-potty stops due to gas and diarrhea. On the positive side, I ended up passing about sixty people. It helped keep my mind amused, even if I was passing many of the same people multiple times as a result of my potty stops.

The bike course involved two laps of a 90 km loop. At the end of the loop were four challenging hills. When I first saw Rod and the kids near the 90 km mark, I was so excited that I didn't realize there was a sharp turn coming up quickly. I almost crashed into the cyclist in front of me before realizing I had to slow down. Disaster averted. I now had some renewed energy after seeing my family.

Near the end of the second lap, after 170 km, I had to make my final potty stop just before dealing with those nasty hills one last time. As I took my bike back from the nice volunteer who was holding it for me during my porta-potty visit, I let out, "I can't WAIT to get off this bike!" He replied, semi-sarcastically, "Yeah, then all you have to do is run a marathon!" The first thing that came out of my mouth was: "That actually sounds really good right now." And that was the truth. I was desperate to get my butt off that bike. How liberating it would feel to run at this point. I didn't care that I was facing a marathon.

The hills were even more brutal the second time around. I was swearing to myself continuously, hating the bike. My butt, legs, and feet were so sore. I saw people on the biggest hill walking their bikes and I thought to myself: *That's what I'll do. I'll walk my bike on that last big hill.* But when I started the climb on the bike, I realized I would be able to do it all without getting off. I was very proud of myself.

The volunteers and spectators from Mont-Tremblant made it such an incredible experience. I saw some of the same people cheering on both of my bike laps. There were some great motivational messages on signs placed by the roadside, such as "Shut up legs" halfway through a hill, or the one written in Quebec slang that brought back childhood memories of growing up in Quebec: "T'es pas icitte pour avoir du fun" (you're not here to have fun). Or my personal favorite: "Pain is temporary, pride is forever."

While I felt a great deal of pain and discomfort by the end of that bike ride, I must say it was distinctly different from the pain and discomfort that kept me sidelined those thirteen years. Perhaps I was able to get past it because I knew what I was dealing with, but there is no question that my muscles and connective tissues were more functional than they had been since my twenties. Everyone feels some sort of pain when putting their bodies through this type of effort. It's a matter of understanding whether the pain is something you can push through or something that requires medical attention. The difference between these becomes clearer with experience.

I thought it would never end. The suffering (at least the bike part) was finally over. Entering transition, I handed my bike over to volunteers and immediately saw Rod and the kids. We shared high-fives and kisses. Awesome. Rod later said he couldn't believe I had such a big smile on my face after that punishing ride. If he only knew how joyful a moment it was for me to hand over that bike. I could have donated it to the Salvation Army in that instant!

Back in the transition tent, I encountered more amazing volunteers. They got my bag and asked if I needed help. I said I was fine and started executing my self-treatment plan by rubbing my lower legs and feet with the Traumeel cream I had packed in my bike-to-run transition bag. The next thing I knew, there was a chiropractor standing over me, offering me active release therapy (ART). I looked at her with a look that said, "Are you kidding me? Oh, yes! Please!" She did the most incredible work stretching out my lower legs and feet, all in less than ten minutes. I wanted to get my ball out and roll the left glute, which was somewhat tight, but again, I would have felt so bad taking my time with all these volunteers trying to help me get out fast. Even with the ART, I was out in thirteen minutes, which is faster than either of my half-iron race transitions.

I really wasn't sure what to expect as I started on the run. My plan was to just keep running until I couldn't run anymore. Except for some uphill sections, that's what I did. Free from the shackles of the bike, I felt light as a feather for the first few kilometers. I was worried about nutrition, however. I really had not eaten enough on the bike. How would I get enough nutrition for the run? The protein bar in my waist pack was not appealing to my upset stomach. Around the 1 km mark, I spotted banana segments at the aid station. Bananas were my staple throughout the run, along with a few gummies, water, and an electrolyte drink. I shocked myself and completed the first 10 km in just over an hour, pretty close to my time on fresh legs! After about 15 km I could feel something burning under my left foot—maybe blisters forming—so I stopped at the first aid tent and put Vaseline on both feet. After that, I just kept running, except for two potty stops. My friend Jean and I crossed paths as she made her way out for the second loop and I was returning from my first loop. I was envious, knowing she would be done well before me. As I approached the end of the first loop, most of the runners around me were heading for the finish line where I could hear the roar from the grandstands. The spectators along the road were cheering us on, assuming we were all heading to the finish, but I had to turn off and head out for a second loop. How I wished I could just stop and go through the finish. Then the words from Jim Rohn came to me: "Don't wish it were easier, wish you were better." *Wow, okay you're right, Jim! I need to suck it up and be a tougher person and finish this thing.* It was actually Rod's voice I heard saying those words, as he had quoted many Jim Rohn sayings over the years.

With 21.1 kilometers to go, my glute muscles were getting tight. I started to occasionally reach back and push my thumbs into the upper glute muscles as I ran. My feet were hurting, but not enough to make me stop. Although very uncomfortable, it was never as bad as what I felt during the marathon in May. It was interesting that my best runs have mostly been during triathlons, which means that the bike must be a good hip warm-up for the run. After a while, my feet didn't really want to come off the ground, so it became more of a shuffle than a run, but I was still moving faster than the walkers. Around 8 p.m. it started getting dark, and there were more and more people walking, or alternating walking and running. Though definitely suffering by this point, I was feeling relatively strong. I felt some sort of psychological victory each time I passed someone, even if most of them were walking.

It was a great atmosphere after dark on the course. A few of the aid stations had music playing and people were dancing. Many of the spectators I had seen on my first loop were still out there cheering and encouraging us. How could I not keep running? With 10 km to go, I checked my watch. I had about one-and-a-half hours to make it in under my goal of fifteen hours. If I just kept running (or shuffling), I should be able to make it. As I reached the 37 km marker (5.2 km to go), as much as I was suffering I knew I would make it under fifteen hours. I was also pretty convinced this was my first and last IRONMAN race. With 3 km left, my body was crying for me to just start walking. But my drive to finish with pride was stronger than the pain and exhaustion. I kept telling myself: *Just run, just do it. It will hurt no matter what, so might as well move faster and get it over with.*

With 1.5 km to go, there was one last hill to walk in order to save my energy for the last glorious kilometer. One kilometer left! Is this for real? Is it really going to end? It felt like I was on empty. There was one last aid station offering water and food. I didn't want to stop. Suddenly I found myself running as fast as my legs would take me. Where was the energy coming from? After a few minutes at this adrenaline-induced pace, it seemed like the finish line was never going to show up, but I couldn't slow down. I just had to keep running as fast as my legs would take me. About 200 m from the finish, the spectators were lined up along both sides of the running path and putting out their hands for high-fives. I slapped some hands until I saw the grandstand full of people. I heard a really loud "Carole," looked to my right and there were Rod and the girls in the front row with big smiles, waving to me. The kids were jumping up and down. A few more steps to the finish. A huge rush of relief, disbelief, and exhilaration. I heard "Carole Staveley, YOU ARE AN IRONMAN" over the loudspeaker. There were lights, music, fireworks, noise. Unbelievable. Immediately, the thought entered my mind: *Maybe I could do one more....*

The next few minutes after crossing the line are a blur. I remember a really nice volunteer coming over to me, putting her arm around me, and asking if I was okay. She walked me over to get my medal, got me a bottle of water, and a blanket. Throughout the entire race, the athletes are made to feel like heroes. That's how I felt in that moment. Now I get it, Jean! Now I know why you didn't stop at one IRONMAN.

Once the volunteer was satisfied that I was okay, she pointed me to the food table and to the place where they take your official photo with the medal. She left me with a big "Congratulations." I was starving, but only half-heartedly grabbed a few food items from the table as my mind turned to finding Rod and the kids. They were back in the grandstand area, but I couldn't get to them because of security. All I wanted to do was hug them and cry with gratitude and relief. I finally saw them behind the fence by the finishers' area. I hurried and got my official finisher's picture taken before joining them. I couldn't stop hugging and thanking them for being there for me, realizing what a difficult day it must have been for them. The kids were totally exhausted and sore from their eighteen-hour day. Arquelle's legs were killing her. She was so happy for me, but the minute we started walking back to pick up my bike and make our way to the hotel, she started crying from pain, discomfort, exhaustion, and the emotions of the day.

I was soaking wet, cold, and hungry and the temperature had dropped significantly since sunset. As much thought as I had put into packing my transition bags, I had not given any thought to bringing a change of clothes for after the race. The walk to pick up my bike, get my bags from the tent, and get to the hotel was altogether about 1.5 km, but it felt like another marathon for all of us. Rod was limping, his left hip flaring up from hours of walking and standing all day. The kids were barely able to move. In thinking about it, this was probably the most draining day of their lives. My feet hurt, but I think I might have been the one with the most energy on that walk, still on a high from the finish.

Back at the hotel room, it wasn't long before the adrenaline high dissolved into weakness and exhaustion. It was now 11 p.m. After peeling off my smelly triathlon suit (it had been through lake water, a seven-hour bike ride and a five-hour run), I jumped into an Epsom salt bath. The bath felt amazing, but by 11:15 p.m. I was feeling really weak and hungry. I desperately needed something with protein, fat, and salt. With all the focus on race preparation in the days leading up to it, we had not planned for this moment and there was nothing in the hotel room that could satisfy my hunger. There were no restaurants open; this was not Toronto where you could have pizza delivered at all hours of the night. Rod mixed Immunocal® protein powder with yogurt for me, which was great, but I needed a lot more than that. The front desk suggested a variety store at a gas station where we might find sandwiches. Rod headed out and found a Tim Hortons coffee shop on the way to the gas station. I almost passed out from starvation and fatigue while waiting for his return. I can't describe how happy I was to see him come through the door with something in hand. In record time, I devoured the best tasting turkey club sandwich ever. Bad carbs, processed meat, but who cares? My body desperately needed calories. I estimated that I burned 9,000 calories during the day. Sleep came easily when I put my head down around 12:30 a.m.

I completed my IRONMAN race in fourteen hours and forty-seven minutes. It was a personal victory to show up at the start line. It is a feat beyond my wildest dreams to have completed it. It is my wish that others with chronic health conditions can find hope in my story and never give up the search for solutions that can take them to their next level.

Make no mistake: I'm not saying that everyone should complete an IRONMAN triathlon. This is clearly not an option for some. However, there are so many people who believe they are stuck in their current health condition, who can't even imagine walking a mile. I want those people to imagine that some day maybe they could walk that mile. And once that modest goal is reached, the doors of the mind could open, and they might have the courage to think: *Just maybe I can take it a step further.*

So what comes next for me? I kept my promise to my daughter and learned how to do a cartwheel. I've now captured my story in this book. Going forward, I will be dedicating many resources to helping people become their own advocates and find the courage to believe that a health problem may not hold them back as much as they may think. Whatever state you're in, there is a better place— whether mental, emotional, or physical. Just SEARCH, SEARCH, SEARCH, take action, and NEVER, EVER GIVE UP! In addition to delivering my message through this book and other media, I am offering a life coaching service for those who are looking for guidance in taking on the challenge of becoming their own health champion.

As for my fitness training and racing schedule over the next few years, let's just say Rod was already at work on August 19 determining what completion time I would need in order to have a chance at qualifying for the IRONMAN World Championships in Kona, Hawaii. Could there be another IRONMAN event or two in my future? Just maybe...

NOT LYING DOWN—Looking Back

Lessons Learned

When it comes to reaching for that big, elusive goal you've dreamt of taking on some day:

✓ Picture the dream, but remain detached. Like a negotiation, your greatest chance of success is when you're prepared to walk away from the deal. Too much emotion wrapped around the final destination can blind you from making progress. Many times leading up to my IRONMAN race, I had doubts about my ability to achieve it because of injury and lack of training. But I was ready to accept the outcome, whether I could complete the race or not. Had I been overly focused on the final destination, I might have quit training at the first realistic sign that I might not be able to finish.

✓ Appreciate every little sign that you might be able to reach your goal, but accept that a million obstacles could get in your way at any time. For example, I celebrated each time I hit a new distance record on the bike, but expected that so many things could go wrong between that moment and race day. When I suddenly got shooting pain in my calf about three weeks prior to the IRONMAN, I was definitely worried and frustrated, but tried to focus on the fact that I was so much further ahead than I could ever have imagined. So what if I couldn't make it this time around? When I looked at how much my health and fitness level had improved, I realized that I had already won. The IRONMAN was the icing on the cake.

NOT LYING DOWN— Looking Back

Health Champions in Action

At one point or another, most of us have been health champions without even knowing it. The message I hope I've communicated to you so far is that we must proactively, consciously, and consistently play the role of health champion in our lives if we ever hope to optimize our health and reach our full physical potential.

The "Health Champion in Action" examples at the end of the previous chapters are intended to share additional stories of situations in which asking questions and searching for better solutions led to a significant improvement in health outcomes. There are also a few examples where opportunities were missed or unnecessary resources were used because the questions weren't asked and the searching wasn't done. If you're not satisfied with the answers you're getting, keep researching your problem, keep asking questions, and keep looking for the right health professional who is interested in problem solving *with* you. Don't expect to take a back seat and wait for someone to find that silver bullet.

There were a few repeating messages in the health champion examples I presented in the earlier chapters:

1. Take charge of your health issue—YOU are the ultimate decision maker.
2. Find one or more health professionals who are knowledgeable AND who are also willing to work *with* you in solving the problem.
3. Do your own research and ask a lot of questions.
4. Don't give up.

It pains me to think of how many people are suffering needlessly because they haven't recognized the need to take ownership of their health problems. Unfortunately, our society has evolved in a way that tends to place anything related to our health mainly into the hands of MDs. Some of us view them as being "in charge" of our health because they know a lot more than we do about medical issues. As much as I agree that most of them have more knowledge about health and medical facts, they do not live in your body; all they can do is respond to your complaints, requests, and questions. They are constantly responding to tidbits of information about what is happening in your body. Very few medical professionals are trained or even interested in looking at the total picture of your health. That is *your* job. MDs and all health professionals are potential partners or allies in our quest for better health, but we need to play our part as *orchestrator* or *leader* in this quest.

APPENDICES

THE NINE KEY STEPS TO BECOMING YOUR OWN HEALTH CHAMPION AND REACHING YOUR PHYSICAL POTENTIAL

1. **Identify what's holding you back.** Have you reached your potential in terms of wellness, fitness, and quality of life? Do you want to be in a better place but have failed to develop a plan for how to get there? Do you have a current diagnosis? Do you think it's the right diagnosis? What does your gut tell you? If the diagnosis is right, have you found all the potential solutions? Be honest with yourself. Have you searched for and implemented everything that could possibly take you to a better place?

2. **Determine your WHY.** Finding and implementing solutions to your health challenges is hard work. The only way to ensure you will continue to push forward despite setbacks and disappointments is to have a very emotionally compelling reason why you want to feel better and achieve more. "To feel better" is not a *why*. You need to go way deeper than that. Picture your ideal life and allow yourself to feel the emotions associated with achieving it; let those emotions drive you to use adversity as fuel to propel you forward.

3. **Build and use your support network.** If you feel like the people you spend most of your time with are draining you of your energy instead of infusing you with positivity, it's time to evaluate who you spend most of your time with. As you start down the path of being your own health champion, you will need at least a few people you can rely on for positive support. These are people who never say never, who encourage you when you set new goals and dare to take risks; these are people who don't allow you to back down when you're feeling low. For me, it's my husband, Rod, and a few close friends. Rod never says: "That's not achievable," instead he says: "What do you need to do to achieve that?" And when I set what seems to be an impossible goal, my best friend, MT, will say, "Wow, what can I do to help you get there?" If you don't have people like that in your life, then find them. They are out there. Gradually reduce your contact with people who tend to bring you down with comments such as "Don't be ridiculous, you can't do that" or "Why would you want to do that?"

4. **Set appropriate goals.** These goals need to be somewhat challenging, but you must be able to envision getting there, even if it's a stretch. Goals must be manageable, so that successes can be reached early on. Celebrate each success no matter how small, and then look to the next goal, which might build upon the previous one. For example, in 2008 my goal was to be able to run 5 km without pain, which I was able to achieve in 2009. The next goal was attempting my first triathlon: a 750 m swim, 25 km bike, and 7 km run. As a non-swimmer and someone prone to chronic injuries, this was clearly a stretch, but part of my brain believed there was a possibility I could achieve it. This first triathlon represented less than 20 per cent of the distances I ultimately covered in the IRONMAN triathlon four years later! But at the time, it was all I could imagine

being capable of. So start small, celebrate success, and keep stretching. Who knows where it can lead?

5. **Find the right health care professional(s).** The one most important characteristic of a worthy health professional is whether or not he or she is a true problem solver. This is someone who listens to your problem and considers all possible approaches to solving it. This person must look beyond their immediate area of expertise and guide you toward various approaches and experts that could lead to (1) the right diagnosis and/or (2) improvement in your condition. You must get the sense from them that they will not give up until they help you. My key problem solver, after thirteen years of searching, was a certified exercise physiologist who looked at the big picture related to my condition. Don't limit your search. Your key problem-solving partner could be a physician, a naturopath, a chiropractor, a yoga instructor, or any other professional in the health field. The critical factor is their ability to consider all aspects of your condition. My exercise physiologist didn't jump into a strength-training program (which is her expertise). Instead she used her general knowledge of physiology and musculoskeletal functioning to determine that there was more to my problem than met the eye. She directed me toward a doctor to perform a blood analysis and suggested that I consult a nutrition expert and a chiropractor. Of course, a customized and progressive strength-training program was an important component, but the outcome would never have been as successful if we hadn't addressed all of the other aspects of my condition.

When searching for a health professional, be open-minded and always have your problem-solving hat on. There are many possible approaches to improving your health status beyond our traditional definition of health care. Reaching a healthier state could involve additional approaches including nutritional analysis and dietary changes, osteopathy, acupuncture, chiropractic care, yoga classes, exercise physiology, naturopathy, psychotherapy, counseling and many more. Although not addressed in this book, it's important to note that mental and emotional health must be strong in order to take on health champion behaviors. Don't overlook the importance of seeking help if you feel that your mental or emotional states are keeping you from taking actions to enhance your physical wellbeing. You can't have the physical wellbeing without the mental wellbeing and vice versa. Keep your eyes and mind open, and always be on the lookout for a new understanding of your condition and anything that could be a potential solution. Being in problem solving mode means asking a lot of questions.

6. **Budget for your health care.** Now that you are the champion of your health care project, you need a budget to implement the project. Good health requires an investment of both time and money. Consider where you currently spend your resources. Are there changes you can make? Go back to your WHY. What is the value of achieving that improved health state? Are there things that you're doing with your time and money that are not critical to improving your quality of life? It's time to redirect those resources.

7. **Implement potential solutions with all you've got (not half-heartedly).** Understand from your trusted health professional *why* their suggested approach might help you and then do it 100 per cent, even if (or especially if) it doesn't feel comfortable. Sort of like reading a book, you can't judge whether it will be a good book until you've read about forty pages. You can't judge the success of a therapy or exer-

cise program by doing it only once. If it truly doesn't help you after you've made a reasonable effort at implementing the approach, then focus on the opportunity in the failure. You've ruled out one thing that doesn't work, which has brought you one step closer to finding what will.

8. **Find every day motivators to keep you going.** For example, identifying music with powerful lyrics has helped me push through those days when I didn't really feel like doing my exercises or my brain was headed in a negative direction due to a setback. While your support network is critical, you also need your own little tricks for those moments when you're left to your own devices. This could also take the form of motivational quotations or imagery. Experiment with different things and find what works for you.

9. **Never, ever give up.** Sure, this is easy for me to say after having solved most of my health issues, but you must keep the faith. There is a way to feel better than you do now. Think about your healthiest state as a journey, a battle that must be fought and embraced every day. It has nothing to do with "perfect health." It has everything to do with WHY you want to get to the next level of health and wellness. Without battles there cannot be victories, so keep up the search for answers to your physical limitations, fight the daily battles to get to the next level, and celebrate your victories along the way! You will be richly rewarded with personal pride, gratitude, relief, and many other incredible emotions that come with winning a worthy battle.

REFERENCES AND RESOURCES

Disclaimer: I am not a health care professional, and the information on the following pages is being provided strictly with the purpose of sharing what I learned through my own health care experiences. The reader is counseled against relying on this information as a means to diagnose, treat, or prevent any health condition. Please seek the advice of trained health professionals (which you've identified following the health champion approach, of course).

A. My observations and insights about interacting with various medical professionals

B. General health and wellness resources

C. Understanding and dealing with musculoskeletal/ myofascial issues

D. Understanding and dealing with infertility

E. Fitness training resources

F. Inspiration, goal setting, motivation to persevere

A. *My observations and insights about interacting with various medical professionals*

What can a family doctor or general practitioner do for you?

I have encountered such a broad range of talent and motivation levels within the general practitioner community that it's really difficult to generalize about them. In my mind, the philosophy behind seeing a GP first is that they can "triage" the various health problems that they are faced with on a daily basis. They should be able to determine whether the problem can easily be addressed at the GP level, or if the patient requires a referral to a specialist or other health professional. In theory, this should work. However, GPs face incredible time pressures as they try to see as many patients per day as possible in order to make a reasonable salary. This is not necessarily the doctors' fault, but rather is a problem with the method in which doctors are paid. They are incentivized to plow through as many cases as possible per day, which doesn't leave much time for listening to a patient's full story about the condition they're presenting with. Nor does it allow the physician the proper time needed to thoroughly think through all the "clues" presented by the patient in order to solve the problem holistically.

The fact that the physician is usually pressed for time reinforces the need for patients to come to their doctor's appointment well prepared and able to succinctly describe the history and symptoms of their problem. I would also encourage you to have some hypotheses about what the problem might be based on your research. If you present your doctor with a "best guess" diagnosis it will at least initiate a conversation about why she does or does not agree with your "best guess." Don't be afraid to ask a lot of questions. If you're not getting satisfactory answers or the solutions offered by your GP are not working, don't hesitate to request a referral to a specialist.

APPENDIX

What can specialists do for you?

As is the case with GPs, there is a wide disparity between the worst and the best specialist in any discipline. Although there is a higher probability of the specialist being able to diagnose your problem, that doesn't necessarily mean that they will get it right. Remember the cardiologist who incorrectly diagnosed me as having pericarditis? In addition, I consulted at least seven different specialists in the early days of my myofascial pain syndrome, with no success.

From my observations, I've concluded that specialists are trained to look for signs of diseases and conditions that fit within their particular specialty area. The assumption is that the GP referring you has done a good job of categorizing your symptoms and that your issues will fit into the specialist's area. For example, my myofascial symptoms could be consistent with some arthritic conditions or something that might fit within the rheumatologist's realm of knowledge. The rheumatologists I saw looked for specific conditions that might be associated with my symptoms. Once the examinations and blood tests came back negative and ruled out their hypotheses, I was sent home reassured that there was nothing wrong with me and given a prescription for anti-inflammatories. This is where I failed myself by taking their word for it that nothing was wrong. Your search must continue. Don't accept someone telling you that you're fine because they can't find any concrete evidence of a textbook condition. Not only do you need to keep looking for the right specialists within the MD community, but you also need to go deeper and reach out to practitioners such as naturopaths, osteopaths, or chiropractors, depending on your specific problem.

What can an orthopedic surgeon do for you?

Again from my experience, I've concluded that once a "mechanical" problem has been diagnosed through imaging like x-ray or MRI, an orthopedic surgeon is someone who could potentially repair the problem, often through some form of surgery.

However, a very important fact that the surgeon might not convey to you is that the real "fix" begins once the surgery is over. The surgery only enables you to do the work to regain the function you once had or to get to a better level of functioning. Assuming a successful surgery, it is the work you undertake with the physiotherapists and/or your strength trainer that will allow you to reach your full physical potential post-surgery. In many cases, there is also strengthening work you can do prior to surgery, which can increase your chances of a successful surgical outcome. If faced with orthopedic surgery, be sure to ask your surgeon what you can do to make your body as strong as possible prior to the surgery, and what steps you should focus on after the surgery to get the best results. If you don't get much of an answer and are given the impression that surgery is all you need, I strongly recommend you seek additional opinions.

The types of questions you should be asking your doctor or any health professional

As a health champion, you should always try to solve problems; your doctor can provide important information to help with your search. Here are some questions you should have on the tip of your tongue when interacting with any health professional:

- Can you explain why...
- What about...
- What is the purpose of...
- What will that (treatment, drug, exercise, etc.) do?
- What side effects should I expect with this prescription?
- What are the risks associated with this treatment?
- How long will I need to continue this treatment to see a difference?
- What other things should I be doing to help myself?
- What do my test results show? (Always follow up after test results, even if you don't get called back to the doctor's office.)
- Can I get a copy of my test results?
- This test result seems very close to the (top/bottom) of the range. Could that be related in some way to my symptoms? What sort of implications could that have for my lifestyle (high level of activity, gearing up for more endurance training, trying to get pregnant, high-stress job, etc.)?
- What other tests might help us pinpoint the problem and give us more direction on finding the right solutions?

Signs to look for when determining if you need another opinion

The responses below are red flags that could indicate you need to see someone else to find effective solutions to your problem.

1. **"Stop doing that."** Remember the joke where the patient says, "Doctor, it hurts when I do this," and the doctor says "then don't do that"? The sad thing is that this actually happens every day in real patient/doctor interactions. If I had listened to the cardiologist who told me to not push myself so hard, I never would have discovered the simple answers of increasing my blood iron levels and regularly stretching my chest muscles. Taking that doctor's advice and looking no further would have meant no half-iron event and almost certainly no IRONMAN triathlon for me. Here are other examples I've heard:

   The man with a partially amputated foot explained to the doctor that he still felt a lot of pain when he pushed down into his prosthetic. He told his doctor that it really hurt when he pushed down on the clutch of his standard car. The doctor's solution: "Just get an automatic."

   The woman who told her doctor that her eyes swelled when she applied eye makeup. The doctor's solution: "Stop wearing eye makeup."

   The young professional, active woman looking for solutions to her urinary incontinence. She liked wearing form-fitting clothes, which don't lend themselves to wearing pads to absorb the leaks. Her doctor comes back with the flip response: "Just wear looser clothes."

   These doctors are completely missing the point by ignoring each patient's individual definition of quality of life. The patient wants the problem solved in order to continue doing what he/

she wants with his/her life, while the doctor just wants to put a band-aid on the problem and get the patient out of the office as quickly as possible. If you can't get your doctor past this type of mindset, then you need to keep doing your research and look elsewhere for help.

2. **"I can't hear you."** Some physicians completely ignore the details you provide related to your problem. The fact that my mother dropped a couch on her big toe should have been a significant clue as to the problem with her toe. Instead, because he saw an inflamed big toe in an elderly woman, the doctor chose to ignore her input and hypothesized that she had gout. If you are faced with this blatant disregard for your description of the circumstances surrounding your problem, it should be a warning signal that this physician or health professional is not the problem solver you're looking for. In certain cases, however, a good physician or health professional might explain to you why your description of the circumstances may not be related to a suspected problem. This was the case when the orthopedic surgeon explained that my chronic symptoms were not directly related to the herniated disc, and that there was another underlying problem that needed to be addressed. Although he didn't know what the underlying problem was, he clearly explained which symptoms were related to the herniated disc and which were not. I didn't get the answers I wanted on the spot, but this was a useful interaction that helped me move forward in my continued search for answers.

3. **"How quickly can I get you out of here?"** Sadly this is the feeling we commonly get during a typical interaction with a physician (and sometimes with other health professionals). The fact is, the more patients they see in one day, the more money they make. However, there is a difference between

someone working efficiently and giving you helpful direction in the shortest amount of time possible and someone who clearly wants to gloss over the problem and get you out, regardless of whether they've addressed your health objectives or not. If you leave each visit feeling like you were rushed out before you could even communicate your objectives, you might want to start looking around. And for those health professionals who charge you directly for their services (non-MDs), watch out for what seem to be "piecemeal" service charges. The chiropractor I saw before meeting Carm was charging me a full fee for each type of treatment he provided. For example, it was $85 for acupuncture and $85 for Active Release Therapy (ART); I had to choose what treatment I was getting that day. Carm, on the other hand, charges me one fee per visit, and I receive whatever treatment(s) I need during that visit. I've received as many as three or four different treatment modalities in one visit, if my problem was particularly troublesome.

4. **"It must be in your head."** In some cases, the health professional might actually listen to your symptom description and do some diagnostic tests that turn out to be negative. And despite your continued complaints about your symptoms, they try to convince you there's nothing wrong with you (thus implying it's all in your head). Trust your instincts. Symptoms are real if you feel them, and you need to keep searching for the cause until you get to the bottom of it. Don't let anyone tell you there's nothing wrong because they can't come up with a positive test result.

5. **"Don't fill your head with all that information."** If you consistently get this type of response when presenting your questions and hypotheses based on research, this health professional shouldn't be included on your team of problem

solvers. A health professional with the right knowledge and the inclination to problem solve should be able to clearly and respectfully address any questions or hypotheses you present to them whether they agree or disagree with the information.

B. *General health and wellness resources*

✓ *The Real Secret to Optimal Health* by Dr. Anthony Galea, 2013, BurmanBooks Inc. Dr. Galea explains some complex but critical medical concepts in layman's terms and gives clear, concrete recommendations on what actions we need to take to ensure optimal health outcomes.

✓ *Inspire Me Well* by Lisa Bélanger and Sarah O'Hara, 2012, Insomniac Press. This book provides excellent perspective on the importance of making good nutritional choices and staying as active as you can within your body's limitations. The authors present several inspiring stories of people overcoming significant health challenges to live their optimal lives.

✓ Reputable websites I turn to for helpful information on most health conditions:

- www.mayoclinic.com
- www.WebMD.com
- www.nlm.nih.gov/medlineplus/

NOTE that these are mainstream health information sources. I use these when trying to come up with a hypothesis to a health problem that is likely not musculoskeletal. If your problem is musculoskeletal (muscle, other soft tissues, joints, etc.), it is difficult to find a trustworthy site with high quality information online. Your best bet is to try and find a good multidisciplinary sports medicine clinic and start with a sports medicine doctor or chiropractor affiliated with that clinic.

C. *Understanding and dealing with musculoskeletal/ myofascial issues*

✓ The following article on chronic myofascial pain by Devin Starlanyl, PhD, was really useful in helping me understand my condition at a deeper level and offered several additional modalities to try myself or ask my health professionals about: http://homepages.sover.net/~devstar/myopain.htm

✓ **Nutrition:** Find a dietitian or nutritionist who specializes in sports nutrition and/or musculoskeletal conditions. He or she should guide you on general principles to follow in order to optimize soft tissue function and should also recommend blood work that can be used to tailor a nutrition plan to your specific needs. For me, the general principles included much more protein than I was eating, about 100 per cent more fish, a drastic reduction in sugar and processed carbs, and a dramatic increase in all things green and crunchy.

✓ **Magnesium:** You should know your magnesium level. If it is anywhere near the bottom of the reference range, I encourage you to take a daily magnesium supplement. Consult with a knowledgeable health professional to determine the right dose for you.

✓ **Omega-3 supplements:** The evidence on omega-3 fatty acids is mounting in terms of their role in protecting against heart disease, eye disease, and inflammatory and other conditions. It is important to ingest these by eating certain fish, nuts, and oils. However, because I want to gain the maximum anti-inflammatory effect provided by omega-3 fatty acids, I take a supplement that is high in pure EPA and DHA, the two omega-3 fatty acids associated with the greatest benefits, in addition to eating five to seven fish servings per week.

✓ **Antioxidants:** Although many products claim to contain antioxidants, the key antioxidant produced by our bodies is glutathione. Maximizing the glutathione in your system is critical to a healthy immune system that can fight off whatever life throws at it. No matter what product you choose as an antioxidant aid and immune booster, verify that it has been clinically proven to increase glutathione levels in humans. The product I've found to have the best data behind it is Immunocal® by Immunotec. You can check it out at: www.immunotec.com. I take one or two packets a day mixed with plain or vanilla yogurt.

✓ **Hydration:** It took a while for me to understand the true concept of hydration. Unless sufficient water is accessing your tissues on an ongoing basis, you are not hydrated. Drinking water when you're thirsty does not mean you're hydrated. Everyone's body has a composition that deals with water and electrolytes differently. I've learned over many years that my body requires not only three liters of water per day, but I also need to take an electrolyte drink each day. And when I'm working out hard and sweating, I need to add one liter of a combination of water and electrolyte drink per hour of workout. I recommend talking to a knowledgeable pharmacist (ideally affiliated with a sports medicine clinic) about high quality electrolyte drinks. The ones most advertised might not necessarily be the best. In addition, I discovered intravenous (IV) electrolytes, which can flood the body with electrolytes that are being depleted faster than they can be replenished with drinks alone. This is especially important during periods of heavy training. I've figured out that part of the reason for my chronic myofascial condition is that my body seems to be naturally low in electrolytes. Endurance training depletes my body of these precious electrolytes, and sometimes the volume of electrolyte drink required for replenishment is too much for my stomach to take, so the IV does the trick. The clinic I go to is called VitaminDrip, and the IVs are directed by a trained naturopath.

✓ **Strength Training Program:** Like I detailed in Chapter 6, it was an exercise physiologist who truly turned things around for me. It was her holistic approach (recommending looking at blood biochemistry, nutrition, supplements, chiropractic care) in addition to developing a strength and flexibility program that took me from dysfunctional to functional. The customized strength and flexibility training program was a pivotal component of my recovery plan, as was Jillian's clear explanations of *why* I had to do all of the exercises that she included in my program. It was the first time someone made me realize that uncomfortable exercises were critical to "wake up" weak muscles and stiff tissues in order to get me to the next level. Don't just find a trainer at your nearby gym. Look for the Certified Exercise Physiologist (CEP) designation from the Canadian Society for Exercise Physiologists or the Certified Strength and Conditioning Specialist (CSCS) designation from the National Strength and Conditioning Association (US). There might be other designations and/or knowledgeable trainers and strength coaches out there, but it is difficult to sort out the true experts without the higher-level certifications. Generally speaking, you want to make sure that as a minimum they have a degree in a physical science like kinesiology, in addition to specialized training for strength coaching. Ideally, they are affiliated with sports medicine clinics and/or sports organizations. Remember, you do not have to be an athlete to hire these people; you just have to want to work with someone knowledgeable enough to have been selected by a sports medicine clinic or a sports team.

✓ **Yoga:** All I can say is you should give yoga a solid try. This means at least one class per week for a few months. Notice how you feel after each class. I recommend starting with the slower flowing classes such as hatha, yin, or basic vinyasa. If you tend to be stiff or inflexible, I recommend a studio that conducts its classes in a hot or warm room. Do your homework on the yoga studio. Ask for the types of credentials the studio requires when hiring instructors.

✓ **Chiropractic Care/Acupuncture:** A chiropractor (especially one affiliated with a sports medicine clinic) is a great place to start for any musculoskeletal problem. Many chiropractors also practice acupuncture, which is one of the treatments that Carm uses on me.

✓ **Frequency Specific Microcurrent (FSM):** FSM is a treatment modality that has helped me immensely. If you're interested in the details of applying the therapy, you can read the book, *Frequency Specific Microcurrent in Pain Management* by Carolyn McMakin, 2011, Elsevier Ltd. You can also find a more layman-friendly write-up to discuss with your health professionals at: www.naturopathic-physician. com/index.php?page=41

✓ **Massage:** Whether it is with a highly credentialed massage therapist or on your own with a roller or massage ball, massage can make a big difference in your life, especially if you're doing the hydration, nutrition, and supplements right. The nutrition and hydration set the stage that will allow your soft tissues to benefit the most from massage therapy. About 95 per cent of my massage therapy is self-administered with a ball and roller. It's great to see my fantastic massage therapist, Tonya, on occasion, but given my busy schedule, it is most realistic for me to do my own massaging at home. I tend to spend about fifteen minutes on it before going to bed. It allows me to get to sleep faster by taking care of the nagging tight spots that pop up during the day.

✓ **Osteopathy:** Although I only recently discovered the benefits of this discipline, a good osteopath can also help you a great deal with musculoskeletal complaints. If you can find an osteopathic practitioner with other credentials (e.g., Registered Massage Therapist, Structural Integrationist) to their name, it's a pretty good bet that they are deep into understanding and solving soft tissue problems. My osteopathic practitioner, Katie Anderson, at Body Vive in Vaughan, Ontario, is one of those gifted practitioners who deeply understands fascial issues.

✓ **Trigger Point Injections:** This is another treatment that could be worth exploring. If you always feel like your muscles are tight and "lumpy" you might have trigger points that could be released with an injection of something like vitamin B12. This would be something worth asking a sports medicine physician or another health professional specializing in musculoskeletal conditions. Mainstream physicians may or may not be familiar with trigger point injections.

✓ **Good Quality Sleep:** If you have been told you snore a lot and/or wake up frequently during the night, I recommend you ask your doctor about being tested for sleep apnea. This will involve a sleep study and a consultation with a sleep specialist. Not only could sleep apnea affect your muscle and soft tissue function, it is also dangerous for your heart and has been associated with reduced life expectancy. This is something worth checking out.

✓ **Epsom Salt Baths:** Whether it's the Epsom salts or the hot water (or a combination), I usually feel pretty good the morning after soaking for fifteen to twenty minutes in a nice hot bath with two cups of Epsom salts dissolved in it. I couldn't find any high quality scientific evidence that Epsom salts can relax muscles or relieve muscle pain, but they certainly can't hurt. The only caveat is that you need to drink a lot of water before, during, and/or after an Epsom salt bath, since I find that the salt water tends to dehydrate. While you might not have lots of spare time to soak in a hot bath, consider using it as reading time. I've never soaked in the tub without a book in hand; it would feel much too unproductive!

✓ **Heat:** In addition to hot baths, I often go to bed with a heating pad on the part of my body that feels tight that day. It makes a difference for me and I encourage you to give it a try if your main complaint is stiffness.

✓ **Ice:** From what I've learned, you really can't do any harm with ice as long as you use it intermittently. Anything that involves musculoskeletal pain can probably benefit from some icing. I can often be seen walking around the house with an ice pack strapped to a body part that feels uncomfortable or irritated, and it usually provides relief. Look for reusable freezer packs and Velcro-equipped cloth holders that you can strap on to the painful body part. I generally leave the ice on for ten minutes at a time. The nice thing about the reusable ice packs is that they warm up over time, and it's unlikely that you will overdo it with the cold.

NOTE After reading the above, you might be telling yourself there is no way you have the time or money to do all the things I'm suggesting. You're probably right. I'm just putting all the options out there so you can start looking into what might work for you. Chances are two to four of the above approaches could be critical for you and your particular problem. You just need to start with identifying at least one and building on it. As for the financial aspect, you'd be surprised how you can find the funding when you identify something that liberates you from pain and discomfort.

D. Understanding and dealing with infertility

✓ *If at First You Don't Conceive* by Dr. William Schoolcraft, 2010, Rodale Books. Although I haven't read Dr. Schoolcraft's book, I can say first-hand that he is an authority on overcoming infertility based on my own struggle with and success over infertility. If I were dealing with infertility today, the first thing I would do is buy this book and use it to formulate questions to ask my fertility specialist. Better yet, I would call Dr. Schoolcraft's office and book a telephone consultation to see if I were a candidate for treatment at his clinic in Colorado. The website for the Colorado Center for Reproductive Medicine is: www.colocrm.com

E. Fitness training resources

✓ *Triathlete Magazine's Essential Week-by-Week Training Guide: Plans, Scheduling Tips, and Workout Goals for Triathletes of All Levels* by Matt Fitzgerald, 2006, Warner Wellness Inc. This is the guide I used to train for both my half-iron distance and IRONMAN races. Although I made many adjustments to the recommended program, it was indispensable in focusing my training efforts on a weekly and daily basis. If you're interested in a triathlon, I highly recommend this book. Whether your goal is just to finish or to win the event outright, there is a program for every level. The only thing it doesn't emphasize is that most of us need to do strength and flexibility training in addition to the swim, bike, and run workouts.

✓ *Coach Troy's Spinervals* cycling workouts. If you own a stationary bike or you're thinking of setting up a trainer to make use of your real bike during bad weather, you seriously need to consider buying some video training sessions. Coach Troy's training programs keep me motivated and force me to push harder than if left to my own devices. You can order DVDs or downloads from the Spinervals website: www.spinervals.com

F. Inspiration, goal setting, motivation to persevere

✓ *The Adversity Advantage* by Paul G. Stoltz and Erik Weihenmayer, 2010, Simon and Schuster. This book makes you think differently about the adversities we face in our lives everyday. Instead of letting these challenges defeat us, we can take them on and use them as fuel to make us better and drive us further. If a blind man can climb the seven highest mountains in the world, what could you achieve by harnessing the power of adversities you encounter on a daily basis?

✓ *Open* by Andre Agassi, 2009, AKA Publishing LLC. If you like tennis, you'll love this book. If you hate tennis, you'll love this book. If you don't know what tennis is, you'll love this book. It's the story of overcoming obstacles, persevering, becoming enlightened, and finding your way in life. A must read.

✓ *What Happy People Know* by Dan Baker and Cameron Stauth, 2003, Rodale Inc. This was one of the first self help books I read after losing my dad in 2005. I wanted to be happy again. This book helped me realize that true happiness has nothing to do with laughing all day long. It's about accepting that everything in life comes to an end and learning to love every moment as it happens more than we mourn its loss.

✓ **My website** includes blogs that might give you that extra bit of motivation to reach higher and take on the challenges that stand in the way of your reaching your next level of physical achievement. You can also check out my life coaching and other services at www.carolestaveley.com

✓ **Inspiring Music:** Music can be such a powerful motivator. Not only should you choose from musical styles that you enjoy, but, more importantly, the lyrics should resonate at a deep emotional level. See my "Believe Playlist" below for song ideas to start building your playlist:

1. *Ain't No Mountain High Enough*—Marvin Gaye
2. *Anything*—Hedley
3. *Beautiful Day*—U2
4. *Born This Way*—Lady GaGa
5. *Born to Run*—Bruce Springsteen
6. *Carry On*—Fun.
7. *The Climb*—Miley Cyrus
8. *Don't Stop Believin'*—Journey
9. *The Edge of Glory*—Lady GaGa
10. *Eye of the Tiger*—Survivor
11. *Feel This Moment*—Pitbull (feat. Christina Aguilera)
12. *Fighter*—Christina Aguilera
13. *The Fighter*—Gym Class Heroes (feat. Ryan Tedder)
14. *Flashdance...What a Feeling*—Irene Cara
15. *Get Up, Stand Up*—Bob Marley
16. *Good Riddance (Time of Your Life)*—Green Day
17. *Hall of Fame*—Andy Wanted
18. *I Will Survive*—Gloria Gaynor
19. *If Today Was Your Last Day*—Nickelback
20. *Inner Ninja*—Classified (feat. David Myles)
21. *It's My Life*—Bon Jovi
22. *Know Your Enemy*—Green Day
23. *Marching On*—The Alarm
24. *Only You*—Yaz
25. *Set Fire to the Rain*—Adele
26. *Shellshock*—New Order
27. *Skyscraper*—Demi Lovato
28. *Spirit of '76*—The Alarm
29. *The Stand*—The Alarm

30. *Stand By Me*—Ben E. King
31. *Strength*—The Alarm
32. *Thank You*—Alanis Morissette
33. *#thatPOWER*—will.i.am
34. *Try*—Blue Rodeo
35. *Tubthumping*—Chumbawamba
36. *Wavin' Flag*—Young Artists for Haiti
37. *Where Were You Hiding When the Storm Broke* —The Alarm
38. *You Get What You Give*—New Radicals

Afterword

Through reading my story, I hope you have found the inspiration, resources and tips that you can start applying today on the path to becoming your own health champion and achieving your full physical potential.

Take charge. Go find what you need to help you conquer your limitations. Cross your finish line, whatever it may be.

And remember, when you get there, be sure to send me your story. I'm rooting for you all the way.

About Inner Victory Coaching

Having crossed her own finish line after years of
pain, Carole uncovered a new purpose and passion
for her life: to help guide others toward becoming
health champions and achieving their best. To reach
this new goal, Carole recently left behind a successful
career in the pharmaceutical industry to found Inner
Victory Coaching, a division of Staveley Enterprises
Inc.. In addition to self-help publications and Carole's
blog offering tips and resources, Inner Victory
Coaching provides life coaching services to groups and
individuals, as well as motivational speaking.

For more information, please contact Carole at:

info@carolestaveley.com

or visit www.carolestaveley.com

Made in the USA
Charleston, SC
25 March 2014